ORIGAMI SCULPTURES

Second Edition

Other Antroll books by John Montroll:

Prehistoric Origami *Dinosaurs and Other Creatures*

ORIGAMI SCULPTURES

Second Edition

John Montroll

Antroll Publishing Company
Vermont

To Jeremy, Rachel, and Josh

Origami Sculptures

Second Edition

Library of Congress Catalog Card Number: 89-081888

ISBN 1-877656-02-X

Antroll Publishing Company

Introduction

This book represents a new direction in origami for me. First, I have made liberal use of new bases that I have recently created, including the dog base and the insect base, which allow me to fold models that are very similar to their real life counterparts. Also, several of the models in this book are folded in such a way as to bring out their three dimensional characteristics. And finally, in preparing this book on origami I have made use of the latest in computer technology, thus blending an art of the past with the scientific horizon of the future. This entire manuscript was generated on a graphics computer, and each page was printed on a state of the art laser printer.

The style of origami presented in this book is the square-sheet, no-cutting method, with the exception of the Walrus, which is to be folded from a dollar bill. The directions for folding the models follow the Randlett-Yoshizawa method of instruction, with some of my own modifications.

For those new to origami, I have included a section that teaches the basic folds that will be utilized in my models. The first four models are designed to introduce the beginner to origami. In addition, each model is accompanied with notes.

Since most origami paper is colored on one side and white on the other, proper shading for each model is indicated by actual shading in the directions. The shading represents the colored side of the paper. This will be important in such models as the Panda and Penguin where the shading becomes an integral part of the model's design.

Although any square sheet of paper can be used in folding these models, the best results come from using standard origami paper. Origami paper can be found at many hobby shops, or purchased from the Friends of The Origami Center of America. The Friends is a tax exempt national organization committed to the sharing of paper folding. For more information about the Friends (books and supplies), send a self-addressed business size envelope with two first class stamps to:

The Friends of The Origami Center of America
Box AB 15 West, 77th Street
New York, N.Y. 10024

I wish to thank the following people for their valuble contribution. I thank Rosalind Joyce who folded all the models which were photographed for the interior of this book. Her excellent sculptured folding technique adds so much to the character of the animals. Robert Lang helped in several ways. As this entire manuscript was generated by a graphics computer, Robert Lang wrote computer programs which enabled me to draw very clear and aesthetically pleasing styles of lines. He also wrote the article on the history of origami. I thank him for his fine work. Also, I thank my brother Andy for his photography and his continued help in the design of this book.

John Montroll

Contents

History of Origami   8

Symbols   10

Dollar Bill   35

Montroll's Dog Base   48

Montroll's Insect Base   106

Basic Folds   140

Swan
Page 12

Diamond
Page 16

Tetrahedron
Page 19

Octahedron
Page 21

Blue Whale
Page 26

Narwhal
Page 32

Walrus
Page 36

Goose
Page 39

Rooster
Page 45

Boxer
Page 53

Scottish Terrier
Page 56

Dachshund
Page 59

Husky
Page 64

Penguin
Page 69

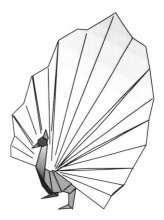
Peacock
Page 74

Horse
Page 81

Bison
Page 85

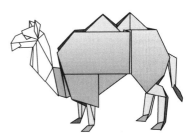
Camel
Page 89

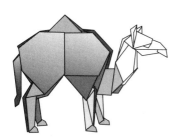
Dromedary
Page 94

Rhinoceros
Page 98

Weevil
Page 113

Asparagus Beetle
Page 118

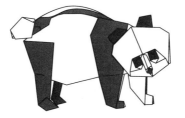
Panda
Page 122

Elephant
Page 130

A Brief History of Origami

Origami, a Japanese word meaning "folded paper," is an art closely associated with Japanese culture. It actually originated in China, however, as did the manufacture of paper. Buddhist monks brought the art of paper-making to Japan in the sixth century, and, it is thought, brought the simplest origami designs as well. Over the next few centuries, while paperfolding languished in China, it flourished in Japan.

Paper was initially a precious commodity, affordable only by the nobility, and was therefore used only for ceremonial purposes. Among the nobility, gifts would be decorated with *noshi*, pleated squares of paper filled with strips of dried abalone; at weddings, the bride and groom's cups of *sake* would be decorated with male and female paper butterflies. Because of its rarity, all paper was held as something sacred; this reverence continues even to this day. The Japanese words for "paper" and "God," though written with different symbols, are pronounced the same, *kami*.

Paper was incorporated into the national religion, Shinto, and paper objects became a part of its ceremonies. Inside Shinto shrines are paper streamers called *go-hei*, which indicate the presence of the deity; folded human figures, called *katashiro* are placed in shrines to receive the deity. The sacred designs tend to be highly stylized, and their folding sequences are rigidly defined.

In addition to the ceremonial designs, many recreational paper folds were also developed. These were passed down through the generations, primarily from mother to daughter. Because they were passed down by demonstration, only the simplest designs persisted for more than a generation or two. Written instructions exist only as far back as 1797, when two works, *Orikata Tehon Chishingura* and *Sembazuru Orikata* were published in the same year.

The term "origami" was introduced in the 1880s. It is composed from the Japanese word "*oru*," meaning "to fold," and "*kami*," paper. Prior to this time, the art had been called "*orisue*" or "*orikata.*"

While its ceremonial function was well established, the adoption of origami as a widespread recreation by the Japanese arose from their embrace of a Western cultural phenomenon. In the 1890s, the Japanese government established a Western-style system of primary education throughout the country, including kindergartens modeled on those of the German educator, Freidrich Fröbel. Fröbel was a strong proponent of paperfolding as a means of building hand-eye coordination, and his ideas met with a wide acceptance in Japan that continues today (one of the larger publishers of children's books is called *Froebel-kan*). Origami is taught throughout the primary schools of Japan and is a widely popular folk art, supported by both government and industry.

Origami spread beyond Japan, over a millenium ago. The Arabs brought the art of paper making to North Africa, and Muslim Moors brought it and paperfolding to Spain when they invaded in the eighth century A.D. They were expelled in the Spanish Inquisition of the Middle Ages, but they left behind their own tradition of geometric paper folds. This became the basis for a Spanish style of folding, or *papiroflexia*. The figures were originally geometric—for Islam forbade the making of images—but after the Moors were driven out, the tradition branched out into representational designs, and a strong school of folding exists today in Spain and Argentina.

Very likely, wherever there has been paper, there has been paperfolding, for in nearly every culture that uses paper, there is some paperfolding tradition. American schoolchildren fold a toy they call a cootie-catcher; their British counterparts make the same shape and call it a fortune-teller or a salt cellar. Even the paper airplane has an illustrious history and can be found in the pages of Leonardo da Vinci's *Codex Atlanticus*. Simple paper toys are to be found in the East and West, but the evolution of origami into something beyond simple toys and stylized designs began in Japan only in the last century.

In the 1930s and 40s, a Japanese metalworker named Akira Yoshizawa began to create his own origami designs. Over the next 50 years, he folded tens of thousands of models and created hundreds of new designs. Equally important, he developed a code of lines and arrows to record the folding sequence for his designs and published several books, which served to standardize his notation over several other competing codes. In the 1950s and 1960s, his work caught on in the West and served as the inspiration for a new generation of folders. In America and Europe, new organizations grew up devoted to origami, and folders on both continents began to invent their own designs and in doing so, took the art in entirely new directions.

In fact, by the mid-1960s, the art was developing as fast in the West as it was in Japan. One of the modern developments was the restriction of the art; contrary to widespread belief, the traditional Japanese designs often used cuts, non-square or multiple sheets of paper. But, as origami designers' abilities improved, there arose an unofficial set of rules governing what was allowed and what wasn't, particularly in the West. In general, an origami figure from an uncut sheet was better than one from a cut sheet; a single sheet was more desirable than two; and a fold from a square was preferred over any other starting shape. This hierarchy was not so firmly established in Japan, where the use of multiple pieces is common and, for example, one master insists that the best starting shape is a 1:$\sqrt{2}$ rectangle—but there is widespread consensus in the West that there is a purest form of origami, and this can be summed up as: one square, no cuts.

Within these rigid limitations, the art has grown to previously undreamed-of levels of sophistication. Today, there are origami masters around the world, and the designs they develop are continually expanding the boundaries of the art. There was a time when an origami designer might claim a particular subject impossible. Far too many "impossible" subjects have been folded for anyone to say that today. Birds, flowers, mammals, fish, crustacea, insects, people, machines, and abstract shapes, all flow from the that simplest, most regular of shapes: the square.

Robert Lang

Symbols

Lines

– – – – – – – – – –   Valley fold, fold in front.

–·–··–··–··–·–··–   Mountain fold, fold behind.

———————————   Crease line.

·································   X-ray or guide line.

Arrows

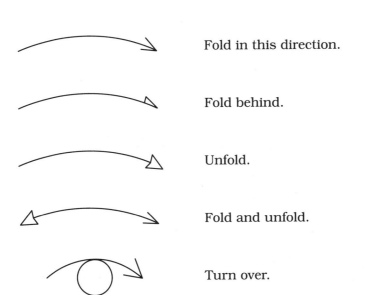

Fold in this direction.

Fold behind.

Unfold.

Fold and unfold.

Turn over.

Sink or three dimensional folding.

Place your finger between these layers.

Swan

The swan is the most graceful of birds. It is four to six feet long and feeds on aquatic vegetation in shallow water. On the water swans are quiet, but in flight they honk.

Two descriptions of the method for folding the swan are presented here. The first description presents every step in detail, the second presents the standard method of instructions, with details left to the experienced folder. In addition, the rabbit ear and outside reverse folds are introduced.

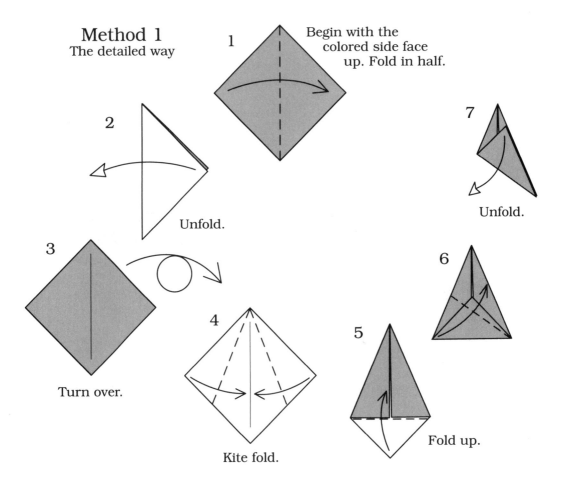

Method 1
The detailed way

1   Begin with the colored side face up. Fold in half.

2   Unfold.

3   Turn over.

4   Kite fold.

5   Fold up.

6

7   Unfold.

8

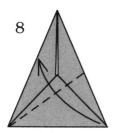

Fold up in the other direction.

9

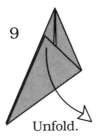

Unfold.

10

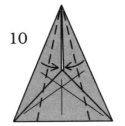

Fold both sides to the center.

11

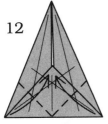

Unfold.

12

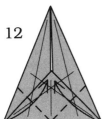

Fold both sides to the center.

13

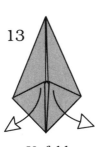

Unfold.

14

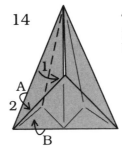

A rabbit ear fold will now be formed. Using the existing creases, fold the long part in half (arrow 1) while placing A and B together (arrow 2).

15

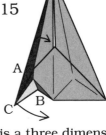

This is a three dimensional intermediate step. Continue by folding C down.

16

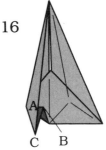

This is another intermediate step. The rabbit ear is almost finished.

17

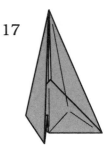

Fold a rabbit ear on the right side — repeat steps 14–16.

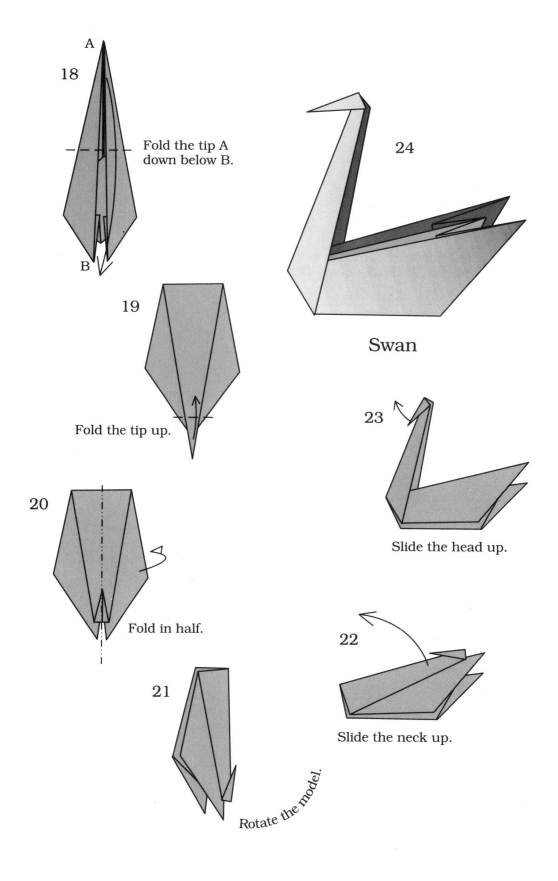

A

18

Fold the tip A
down below B.

B

19

Fold the tip up.

20

Fold in half.

21

Rotate the model.

22

Slide the neck up.

23

Slide the head up.

24

Swan

Method 2
The standard way

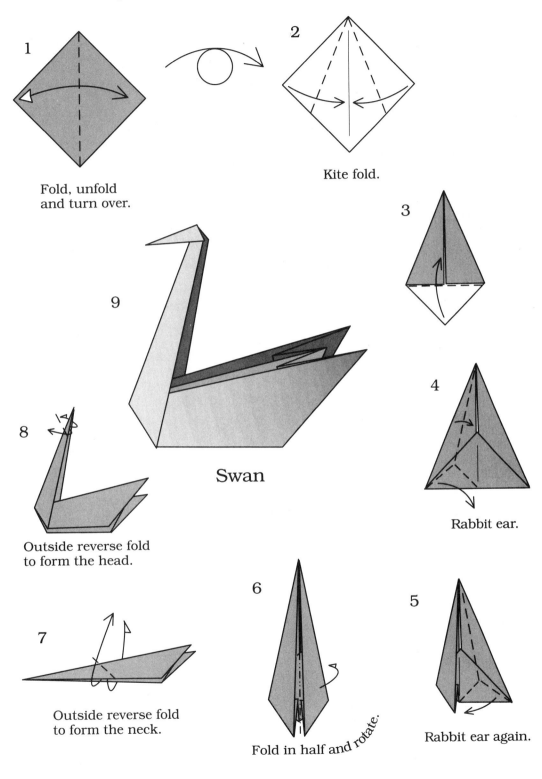

1 Fold, unfold and turn over.

2 Kite fold.

3

4 Rabbit ear.

5 Rabbit ear again.

6 Fold in half and rotate.

7 Outside reverse fold to form the neck.

8 Outside reverse fold to form the head.

9

Swan

Diamond

This three dimensional geometric shape makes an elegant ornament. It is formed from the Preliminary Fold, which is a common starting shape for many origami designs. A detailed method for making the Preliminary Fold is shown.

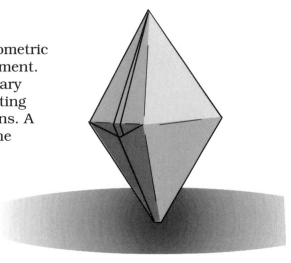

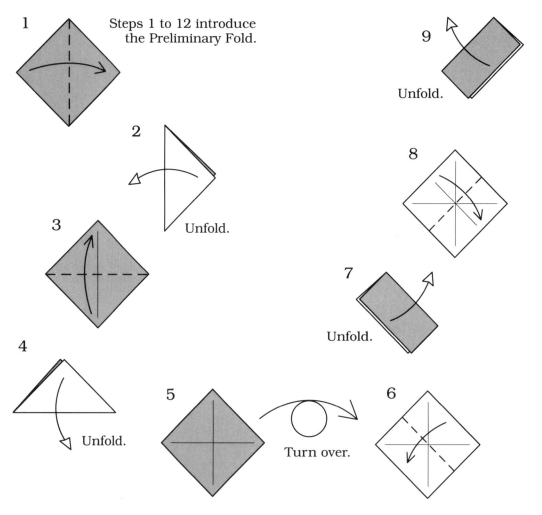

1

Steps 1 to 12 introduce the Preliminary Fold.

2

Unfold.

3

4

Unfold.

5

Turn over.

6

7

Unfold.

8

9

Unfold.

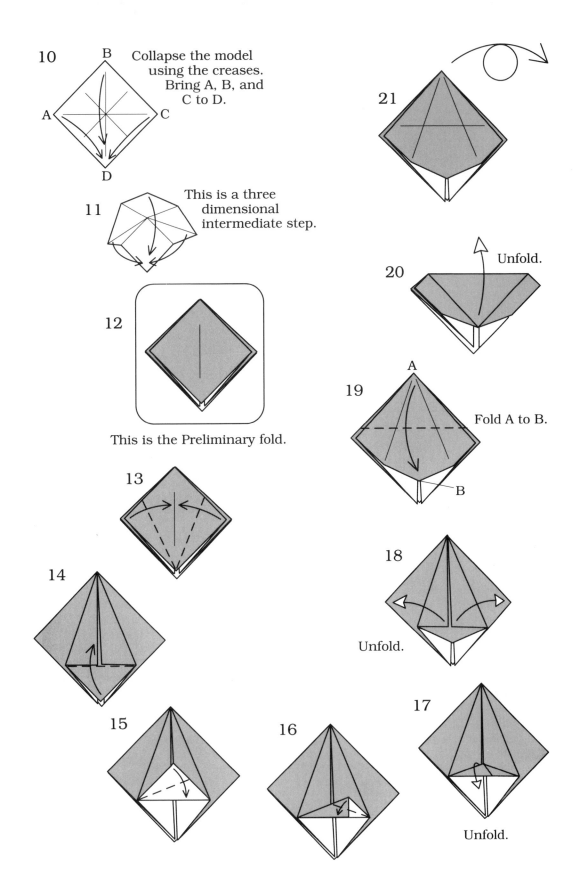

10 B Collapse the model using the creases. Bring A, B, and C to D.

A C

D

11 This is a three dimensional intermediate step.

12 This is the Preliminary fold.

13

14

15

16

17 Unfold.

18 Unfold.

19 A Fold A to B. B

20 Unfold.

21

22

Repeat steps 13 to 18.

23

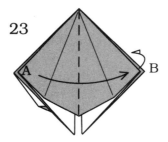

Fold A to the right and
B behind to the left.

24

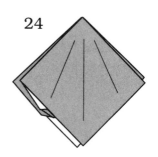

Repeat steps 14 to 18
on the front and back.

25

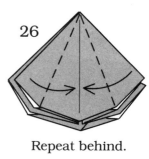

26

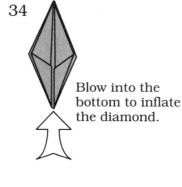

Repeat behind.

33

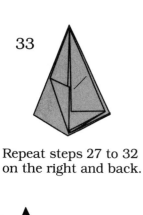

Repeat steps 27 to 32
on the right and back.

34

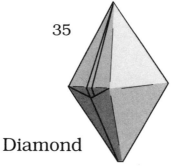

Blow into the
bottom to inflate
the diamond.

32

Tuck inside.

35

Diamond

31

30

Unfold.

29

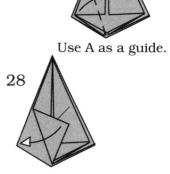

27

A

Use A as a guide.

28

Unfold.

Tetrahedron

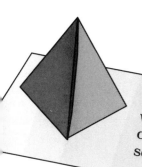

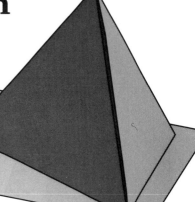

This three dimensional shape has four sides, each an equilateral triangle. We start with simple valley folds. Then come more complicated steps to make the sculpture three dimensional.

1

Fold in half.

2

Unfold.

3

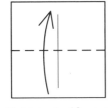

Fold in half again.

4

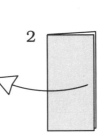

Unfold.

5

B — C

A

Fold corner A to the line B–C, close to C.

6

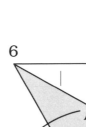

A — C

Unfold.

7

B — C — D

Fold corner D to the line B–C, close to B.

8

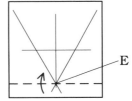

Unfold.

9

E

Fold up using point E as a guide.

10

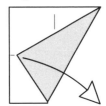

Fold in half.

11

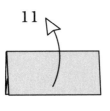

Unfold.

12

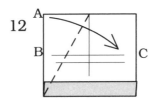

Fold corner A to the line B–C, close to C.

13

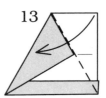

14

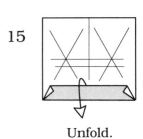

Unfold.

20

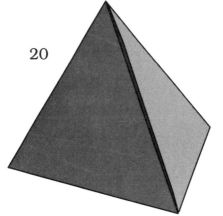

Tetrahedron

15

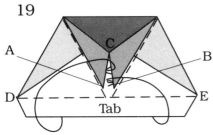

Unfold.

19

In this three dimensional drawing, corner C is coming out of the page. Fold D and E up to C and tuck the long tab inside.

16

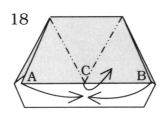

While folding the line A–B down, fold the edges C and D inside. Fold on the existing creases.

17

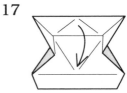

This is a three dimensional intermediate step.

18

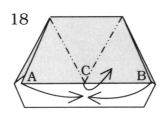

Lift C up! Bring A and B together.

Octahedron

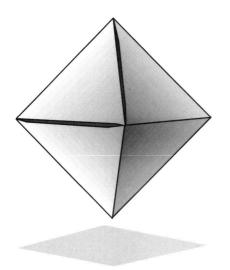

This three dimensional shape has eight sides, each an equilateral triangle. The folding method uses the waterbomb base, a common pattern for beginning many origami models.

1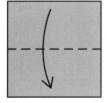

Begin with the colored side face up. Fold in half.

2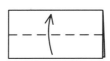

Fold up.

3

Turn over.

4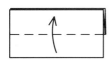

Fold up.

5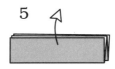

Unfold everything.

6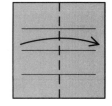

Fold in half.

7

Fold in half and repeat behind.

8

Unfold everything.

9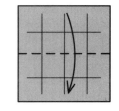

Fold in half again.

10

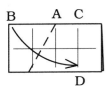

Using A as a guide, fold B to the line C–D, close to D.

11

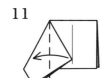

Fold in half.

12

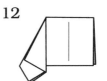

Turn over.

13

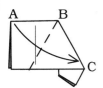

Fold A to the line B–C, close to C.

14

Fold in half.

15

Unfold everything.

16

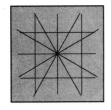

Turn over.

17

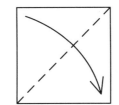

Fold diagonally in half.

18

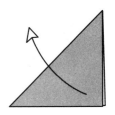

Unfold.

19

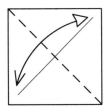

Fold and unfold.

20

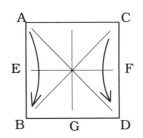

Collapse the paper on the creases shown. A will go to B, C to D, and E and F to G.

21

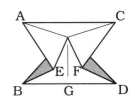

This is a three dimensional intermediate step.

22

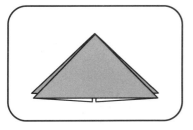

This is the
Waterbomb Base.

23

Reverse fold on the existing crease.
To do this, place your finger all the
way inside the model and push the
region, shown as a darker grey,
inside the model.

24

This is a three dimensional
intermediate step.

25

Make the same reverse fold on
the three other sides. (Repeat
steps 23–24 on those sides.)

26

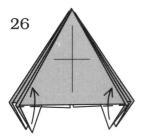

Fold the white triangles
up. Repeat behind.

27

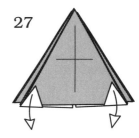

Fold the triangles down.
Repeat behind.

28

Fold the triangles back
up but tuck them under
the darker front layer.
Repeat behind.

29

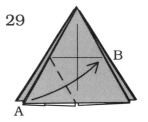

Fold A to B.

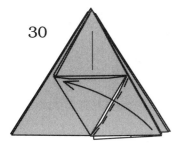

30

Fold up.

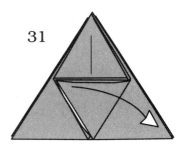

31

Unfold.

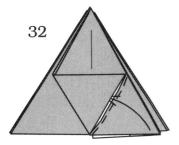

32

Tuck inside the pocket.

33

Turn over.

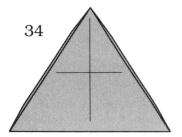

34

Repeat steps 29–33.

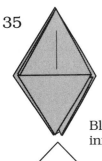

35

Blow into the bottom to inflate the octahedron.

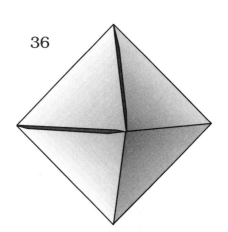

36

Octahedron

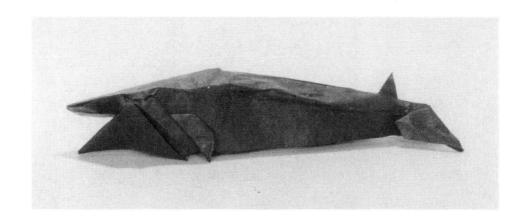

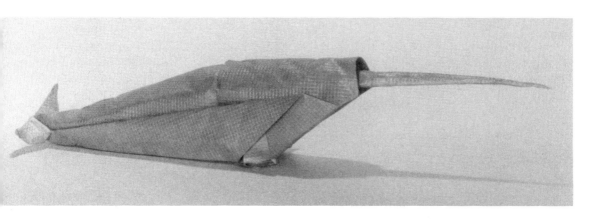

Blue Whale

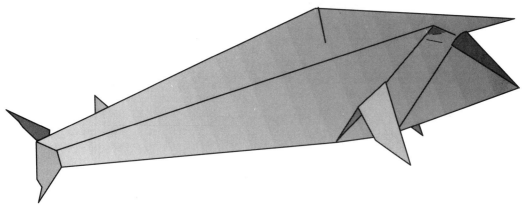

This is the largest animal in the world. The blue whale is 100 feet long and weighs over 150 tons. It spends the summers in polar waters eating over four tons of small shrimp a day. During the winter it swims towards the equator to breed.

The blue whale is a baleen whale. Baleen whales have no teeth but instead, hundreds of plates in the mouth which hang from the upper jaw. The plates, called baleen, strain out food from the water.

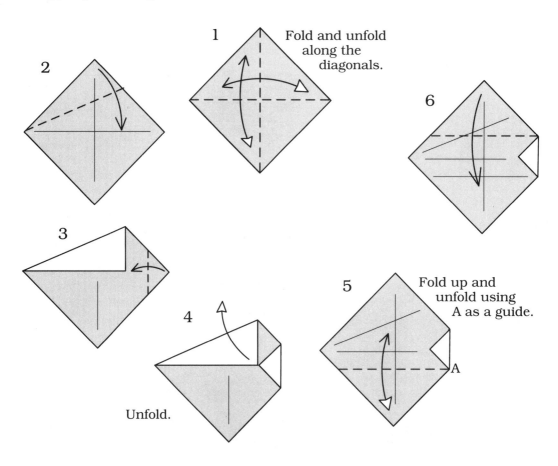

1 Fold and unfold along the diagonals.

2

3

4 Unfold.

5 Fold up and unfold using A as a guide.

A

6

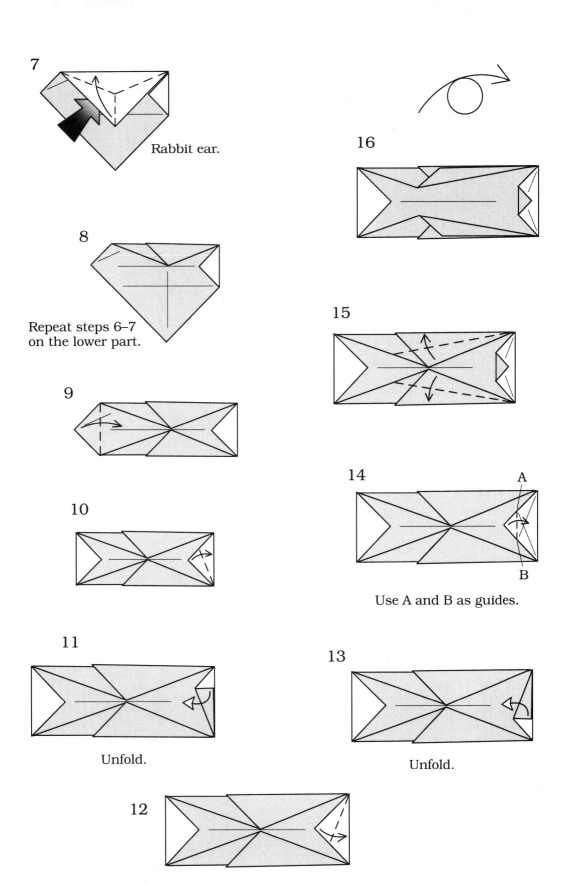

7

Rabbit ear.

8

Repeat steps 6–7 on the lower part.

9

10

11

Unfold.

12

16

15

14

Use A and B as guides.

A

B

13

Unfold.

17

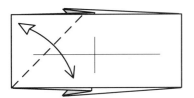

Fold and unfold.

26

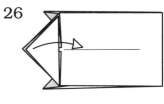

Unfold.

18

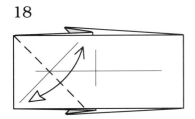

Fold and unfold.

25

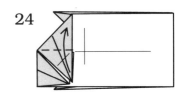

Repeat steps 20–24.

19

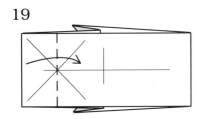

24

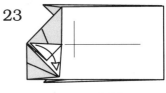

20

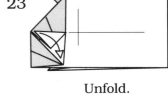

The squash fold is introduced.
Place your finger as shown by
the large arrow.

23

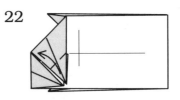

Unfold.

21

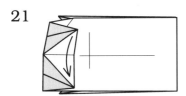

This is a three dimensional
intermediate step.

22

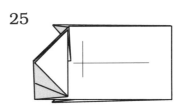

ORIGAMI SCULPTURES

27

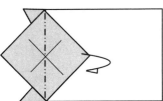

28

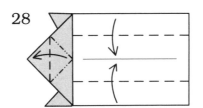

One form of the petal
fold is introduced.

29

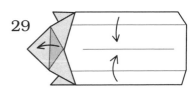

A three dimensional
intermediate step.

31

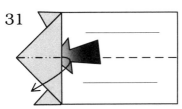

This is similar to a squash fold.

30

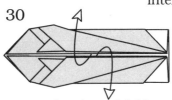

A completed petal fold.
Unfold it (back to step 28).

32

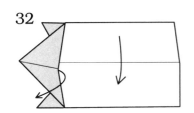

A three dimensional
intermediate step.

35

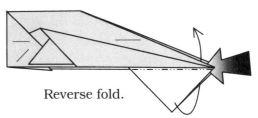

Reverse fold.

33

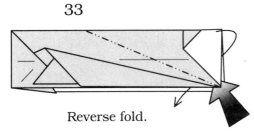

Reverse fold.

34

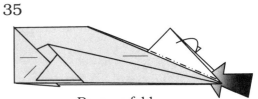

Reverse fold.

36

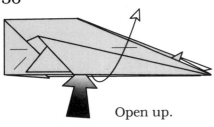

Open up.

37

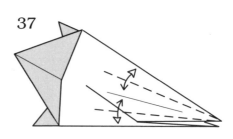

This is a three dimensional figure. Fold and unfold.

38

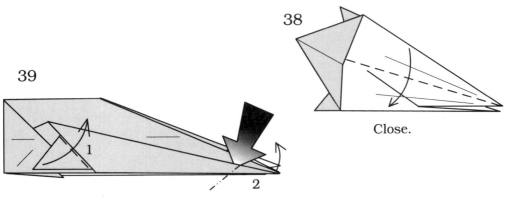

Close.

39

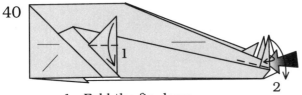

1. Fold the fin up.
2. Reverse fold the tail.
Repeat behind.

40

1. Fold the fin down.
2. Make a little squash fold for the tail.
Repeat behind.

41

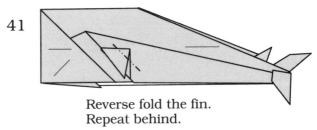

Reverse fold the fin.
Repeat behind.

42

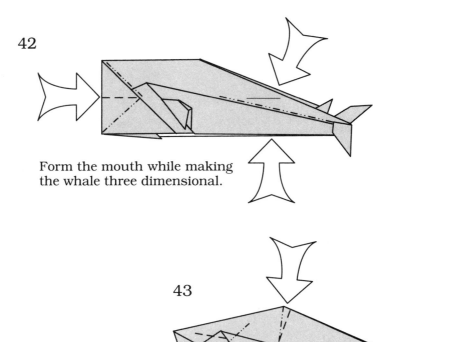

Form the mouth while making
the whale three dimensional.

43

Form the eyes while
folding the mouth down.

44

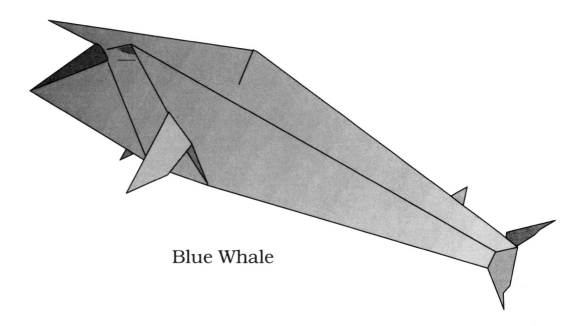

Blue Whale

Narwhal

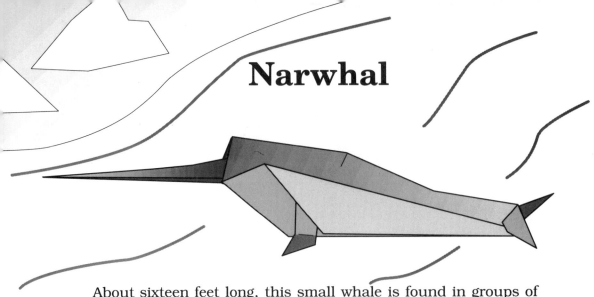

About sixteen feet long, this small whale is found in groups of 15–20 along the Arctic coasts and rivers north of Alaska. It has only two teeth, which grow from the tip of the upper jaw. The male narwhal's left tooth grows straight out to form the nine foot tusk. It eats crabs, shrimp, squid, and fish.

1

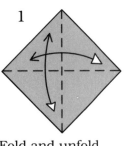

Fold and unfold along the diagonals.

2

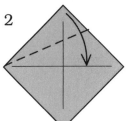

3

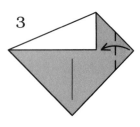

4

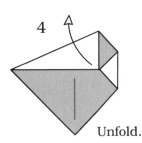

Unfold.

5

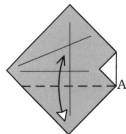

Fold up and unfold using A as a guide.

6

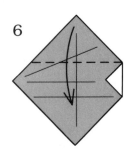

7

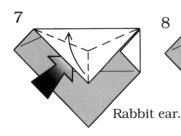

Rabbit ear.

8

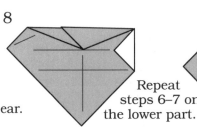

Repeat steps 6–7 on the lower part.

9

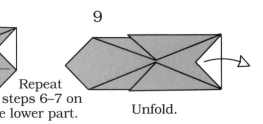

Unfold.

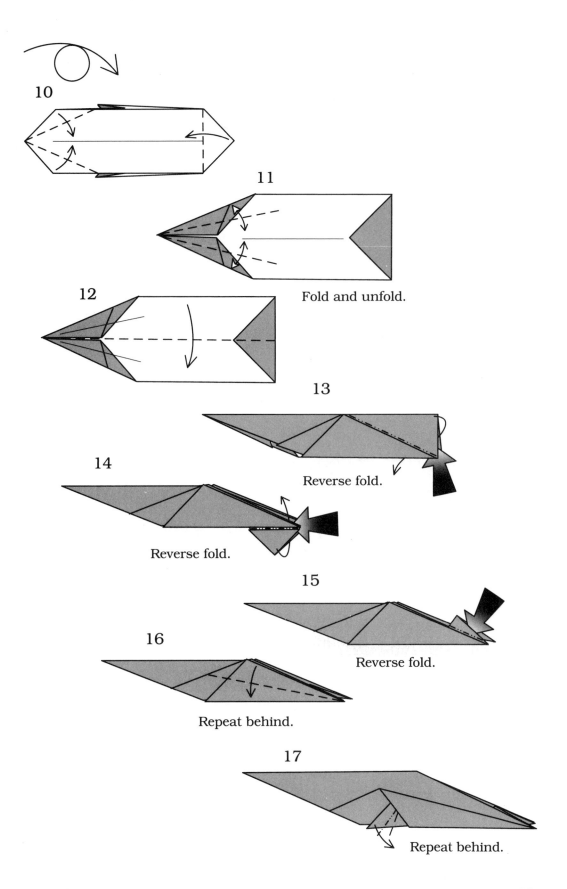

10

11

Fold and unfold.

12

13

Reverse fold.

14

Reverse fold.

15

Reverse fold.

16

Repeat behind.

17

Repeat behind.

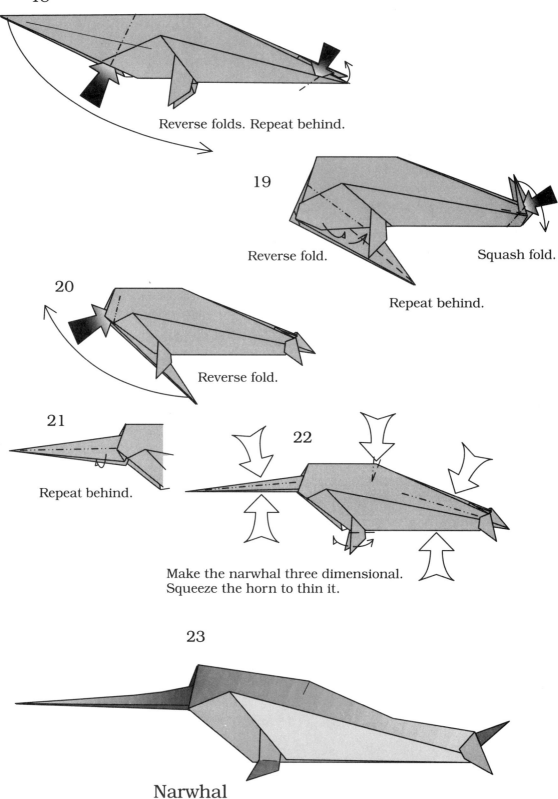

18

Reverse folds. Repeat behind.

19

Reverse fold.

Squash fold.

Repeat behind.

20

Reverse fold.

21

Repeat behind.

22

Make the narwhal three dimensional.
Squeeze the horn to thin it.

23

Narwhal

ORIGAMI SCULPTURES

Dollar Bill

This shows how to convert a
square into two rectangles
which each have the
proportions of a dollar bill.
It can be used to fold the
walrus (next model).

1

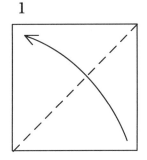

2

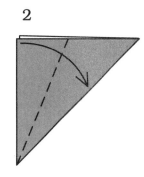

3

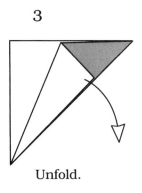

Unfold.

4

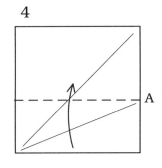

A

Fold up using A
as a guide.

5

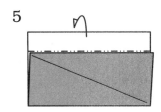

6

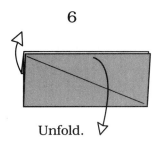

Unfold.

7

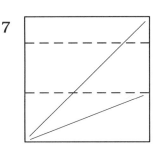

Cut along the dotted lines.
The two larger rectangles
have the proportions of a
dollar bill.

8

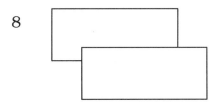

Dollar Bills

Walrus

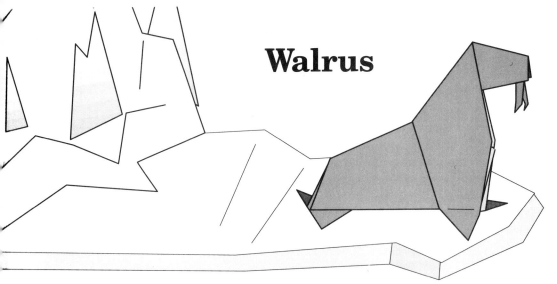

This mammal lives on ice floes in the North Altantic, North Pacific and Arctic Oceans. It is about eleven feet long and weighs 3000 pounds. With its tusks, it can dig up mollusks, crustaceans, and fish to eat.

These social animals spend much of their time resting and sleeping in the sun. They hate to be disturbed while sleeping. A walrus that is hit accidentally by another one's flipper will make a sound and hit another walrus. Then all would hit each other until they finally go back to sleep.

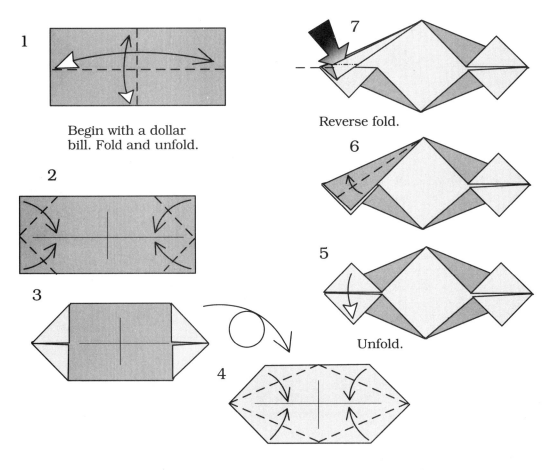

1

Begin with a dollar bill. Fold and unfold.

2

3

4

5

Unfold.

6

7

Reverse fold.

8

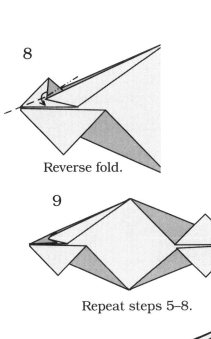

Reverse fold.

9

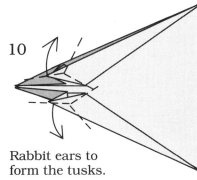

Repeat steps 5–8.

10

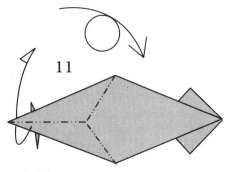

Rabbit ears to
form the tusks.

11

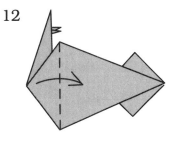

Rabbit ear.

12

13

16

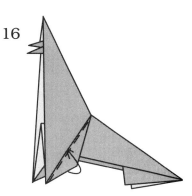

Tuck inside. Repeat behind.

15

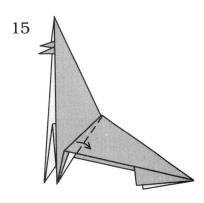

Repeat behind.

The outside crimp fold
is introduced. A
crimp fold is symmetric
with respect to the
front and back. Pivot
around A.

14

A

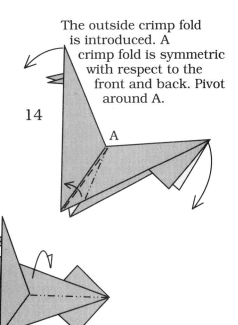

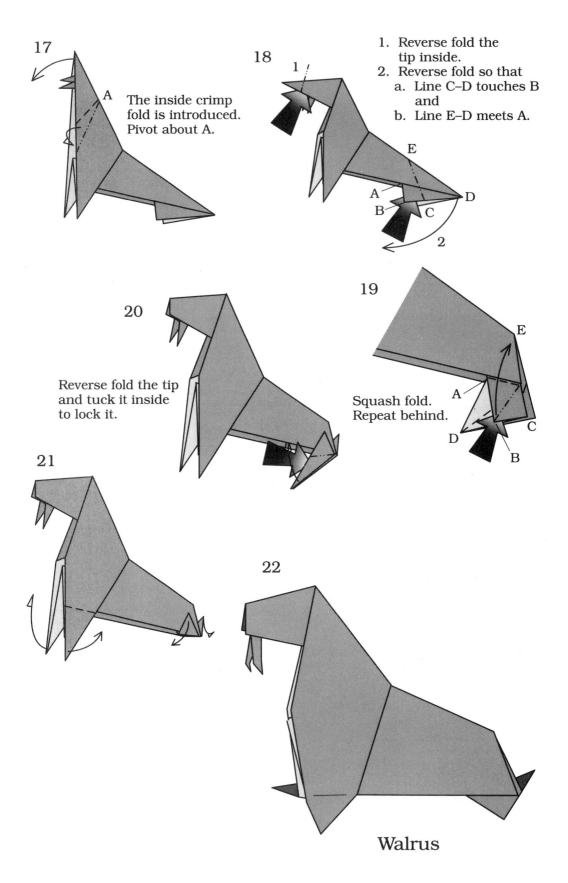

17 The inside crimp fold is introduced. Pivot about A.

18
1. Reverse fold the tip inside.
2. Reverse fold so that
   a. Line C–D touches B and
   b. Line E–D meets A.

19 Squash fold. Repeat behind.

20 Reverse fold the tip and tuck it inside to lock it.

21

22

Walrus

Goose

About two to three feet tall, these web-footed birds are closely related to the duck and swan. They migrate north in summer and south in winter, often flying in a line or V formation while honking energetically. Large flocks are found in grassy marshes and in grain fields. Geese eat grasses, seeds, and aquatic plants.

1

Fold and unfold along the diagonals.

2

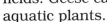

Fold and unfold.

3

C

B←·—·—×—·—·→D

A

Collapse along the creases so that corners B, C, and D lie on top of A.

4

This is the Preliminary Fold. Kite fold.

5

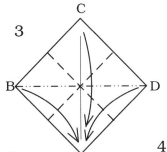

The folding and unfolding in steps 4–6 prepare for the petal fold. While doing the petal fold (steps 7–10) only fold upon the creases formed from steps 4–5.

6

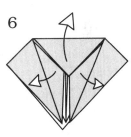

Unfold.

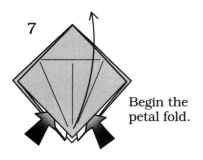

7

Begin the petal fold.

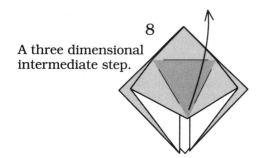

8

A three dimensional intermediate step.

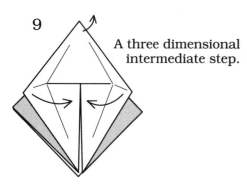

9

A three dimensional intermediate step.

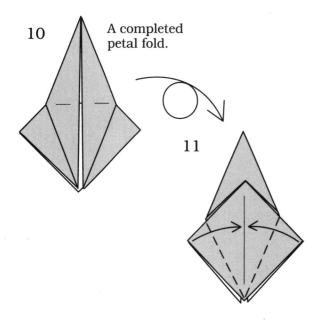

10

A completed petal fold.

11

12

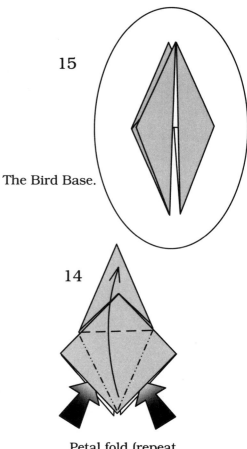

15

The Bird Base.

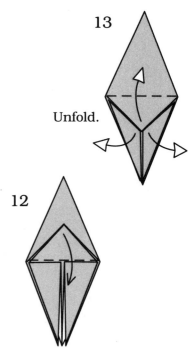

14

Petal fold (repeat steps 7–10).

13

Unfold.

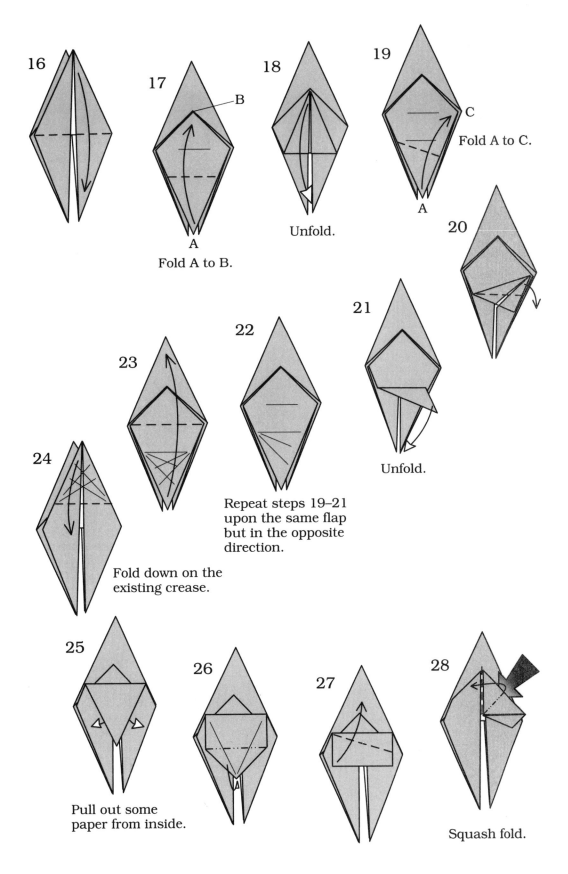

16

17

B

18

19

C

Fold A to C.

A

Fold A to B.

A

Unfold.

20

21

Unfold.

22

Repeat steps 19–21 upon the same flap but in the opposite direction.

23

24

Fold down on the existing crease.

25

Pull out some paper from inside.

26

27

28

Squash fold.

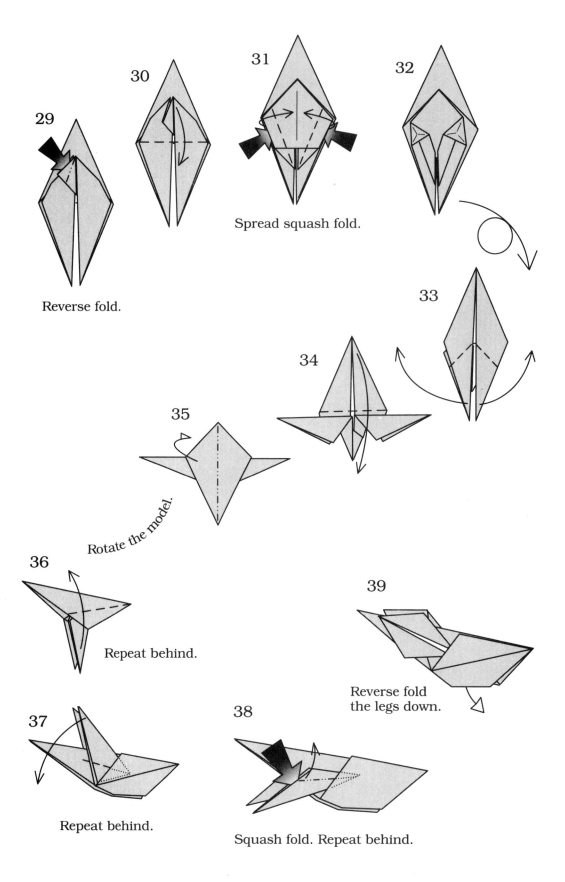

29

Reverse fold.

30

31

Spread squash fold.

32

33

34

35

Rotate the model.

36

Repeat behind.

37

Repeat behind.

38

Squash fold. Repeat behind.

39

Reverse fold
the legs down.

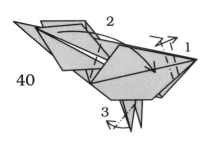

40

1. Crimp fold the tail.
2. Fold the wings down. Repeat behind.
3. Reverse fold the feet. Repeat behind.

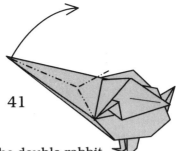

41

The double rabbit ear is introduced. This fold is symmetric with respect to the front and back.

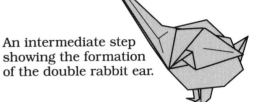

42

An intermediate step showing the formation of the double rabbit ear.

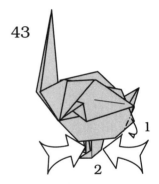

43

1. Fold behind, repeat behind.
2. Squeeze the legs and flatten the feet so the goose can stand.

48

Goose

47

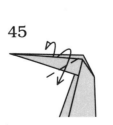

Crimp fold to form the beak.

46

Pull out some paper from inside to make the head wider. Repeat behind.

45

Outside reverse fold.

44 Head.

Reverse fold.

ORIGAMI SCULPTURES

Rooster

This is the adult male chicken. Roosters developed from the wild red jungle fowl of India and have been domesticated for 5000 years. Roosters had been used for fighting and show.

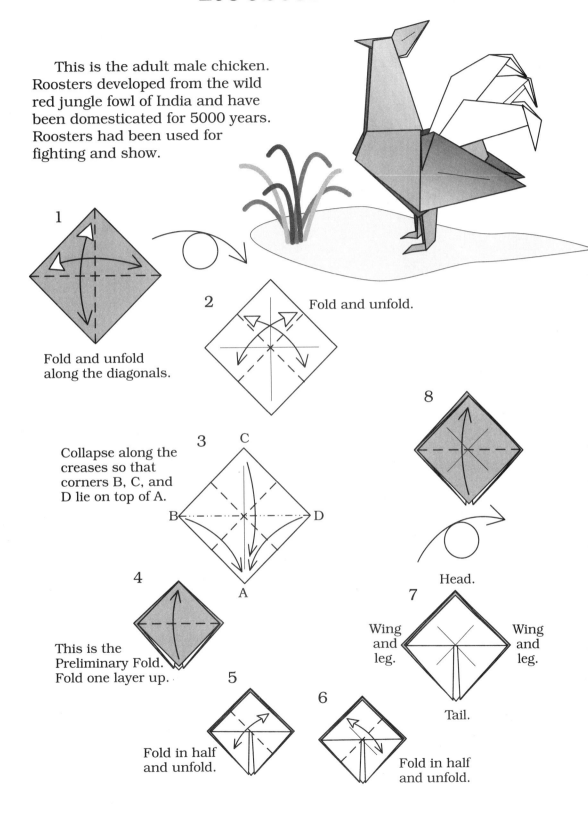

1 Fold and unfold along the diagonals.

2 Fold and unfold.

3 Collapse along the creases so that corners B, C, and D lie on top of A.

C

B   D

A

4 This is the Preliminary Fold. Fold one layer up.

5 Fold in half and unfold.

6 Fold in half and unfold.

7 Head.

Wing and leg.   Wing and leg.

Tail.

8

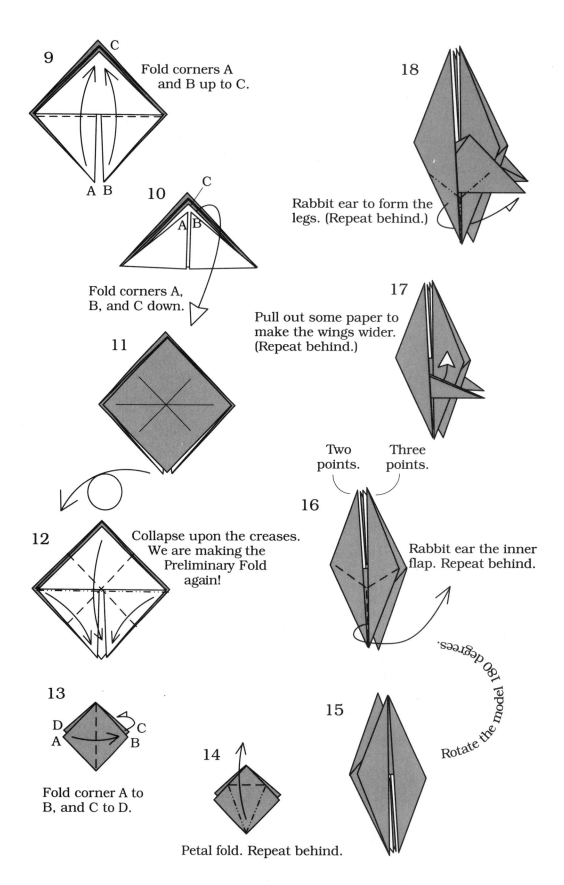

9 Fold corners A and B up to C.

10 Fold corners A, B, and C down.

11

Collapse upon the creases. We are making the Preliminary Fold again!

12

13 Fold corner A to B, and C to D.

14 Petal fold. Repeat behind.

15

Rotate the model 180 degrees.

16 Rabbit ear the inner flap. Repeat behind.

Two points. Three points.

17 Pull out some paper to make the wings wider. (Repeat behind.)

18 Rabbit ear to form the legs. (Repeat behind.)

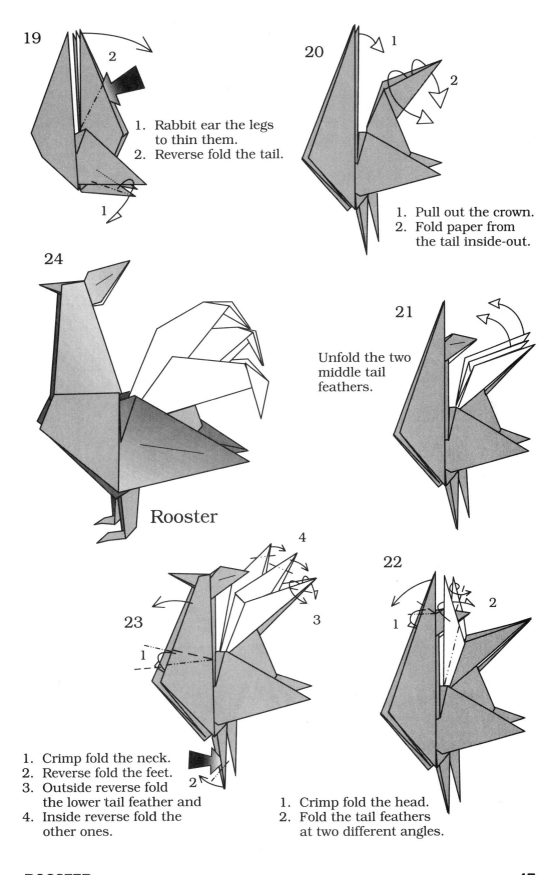

19

1. Rabbit ear the legs to thin them.
2. Reverse fold the tail.

20

1. Pull out the crown.
2. Fold paper from the tail inside-out.

21

Unfold the two middle tail feathers.

22

1. Crimp fold the head.
2. Fold the tail feathers at two different angles.

23

1. Crimp fold the neck.
2. Reverse fold the feet.
3. Outside reverse fold the lower tail feather and
4. Inside reverse fold the other ones.

24

Rooster

Montroll's Dog Base

Many four-legged animals can be folded from this base which are larger in comparison to other folding methods. They are not thick, they hold together well, have impressive head detail, are well proportioned, and have a three dimensional sculptural effect.

Several animals in this book use this base and variations of it. When I first developed it I created several dogs, some included in this volume — hence the name "Dog Base".

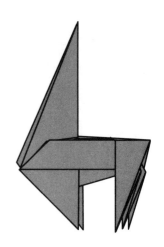

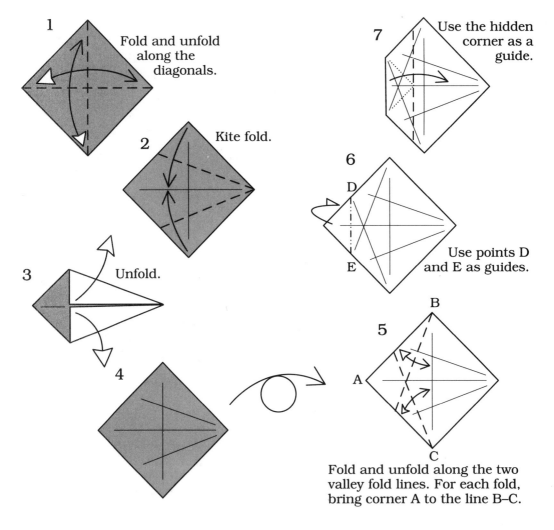

1 Fold and unfold along the diagonals.

2 Kite fold.

3 Unfold.

4

5 Fold and unfold along the two valley fold lines. For each fold, bring corner A to the line B–C.

6 Use points D and E as guides.

7 Use the hidden corner as a guide.

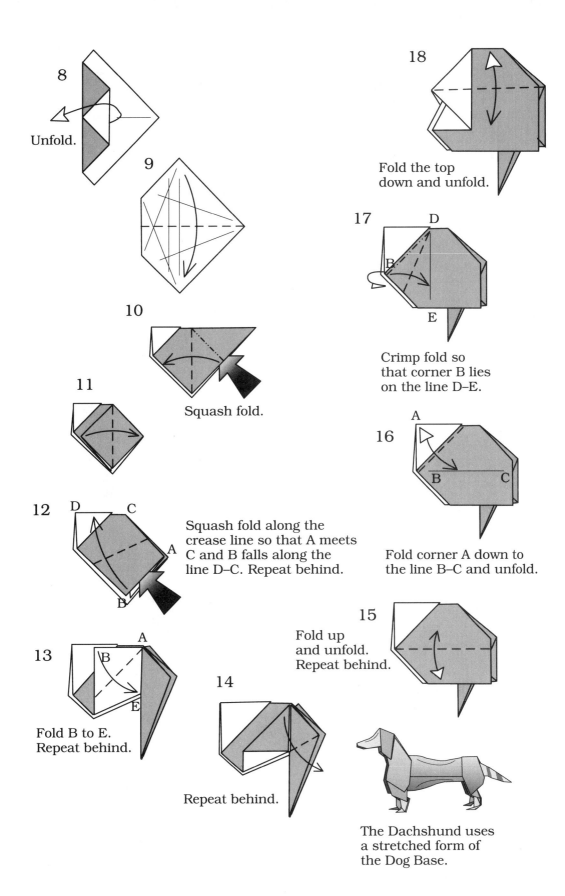

8

Unfold.

9

10

11

Squash fold.

12

D   C

A

B

Squash fold along the crease line so that A meets C and B falls along the line D–C. Repeat behind.

13

A

B

E

Fold B to E.
Repeat behind.

14

Repeat behind.

15

Fold up
and unfold.
Repeat behind.

16

A

B   C

Fold corner A down to the line B–C and unfold.

17

D

B

E

Crimp fold so that corner B lies on the line D–E.

18

Fold the top down and unfold.

The Dachshund uses a stretched form of the Dog Base.

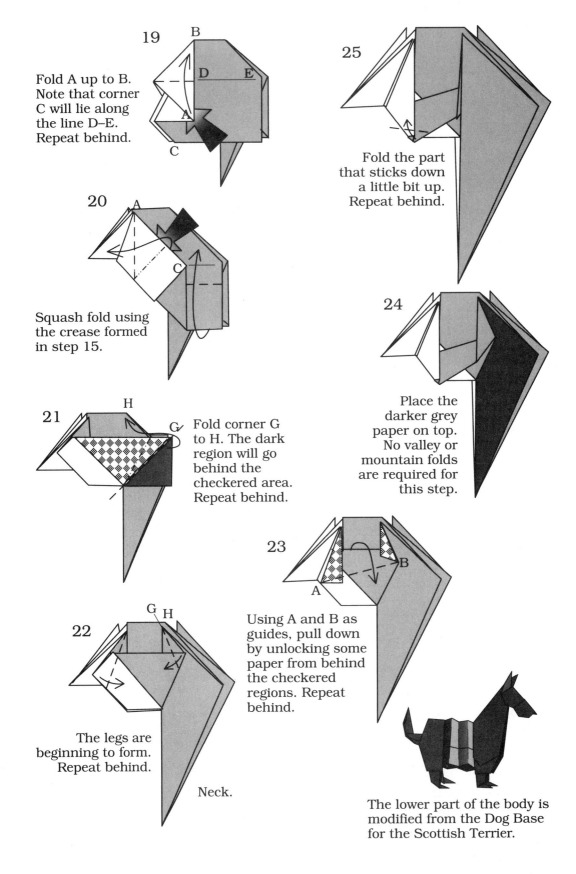

19

Fold A up to B. Note that corner C will lie along the line D–E. Repeat behind.

20

Squash fold using the crease formed in step 15.

21

Fold corner G to H. The dark region will go behind the checkered area. Repeat behind.

22

The legs are beginning to form. Repeat behind.

Neck.

23

Using A and B as guides, pull down by unlocking some paper from behind the checkered regions. Repeat behind.

24

Place the darker grey paper on top. No valley or mountain folds are required for this step.

25

Fold the part that sticks down a little bit up. Repeat behind.

The lower part of the body is modified from the Dog Base for the Scottish Terrier.

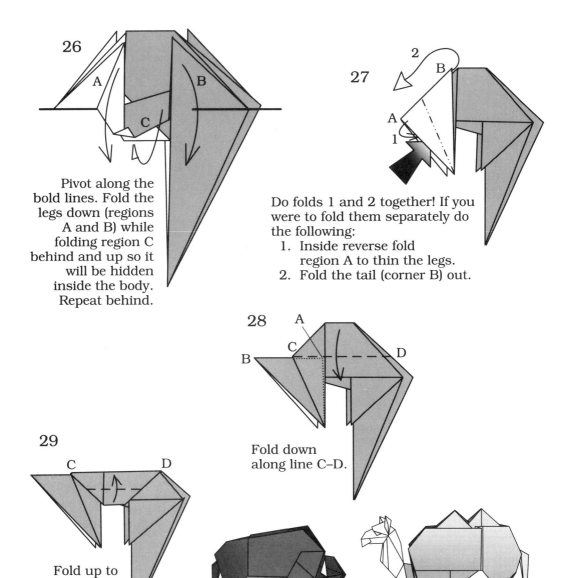

26

A B C

Pivot along the bold lines. Fold the legs down (regions A and B) while folding region C behind and up so it will be hidden inside the body. Repeat behind.

27

2 B A 1

Do folds 1 and 2 together! If you were to fold them separately do the following:
1. Inside reverse fold region A to thin the legs.
2. Fold the tail (corner B) out.

28

A C B D

Fold down along line C–D.

29

C D

Fold up to line C–D.

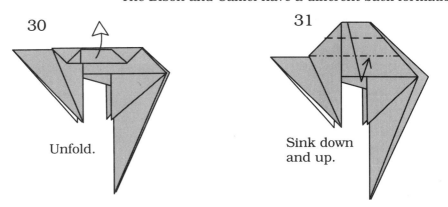

The Bison and Camel have a different back formation.

30

Unfold.

31

Sink down and up.

32

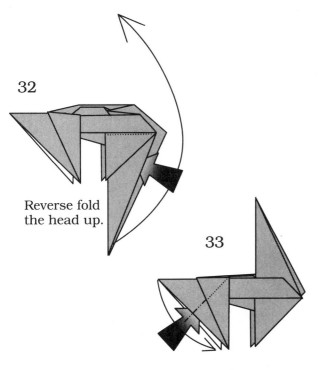

Reverse fold
the head up.

33

Reverse fold the tail down.

The Horse has a
different tail formation.

34

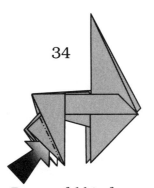

Reverse fold to form
the back legs and tail.
Repeat behind.

35

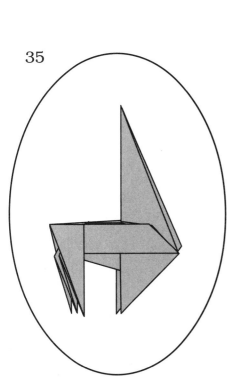

Montroll's Dog Base

The Boxer is from the Dog Base.

ORIGAMI SCULPTURES

Boxer

This medium-sized noble dog is one of the most popular working breeds. It is used in police work because it is intelligent and aggressive. It is playful and gentle, making it a good family dog. It was named because of the way it appearred to be boxing with its front paws when it would begin to fight. It is about two feet high at the shoulder and weighs 60 to 70 pounds.

Begin with the Dog Base (page 48).

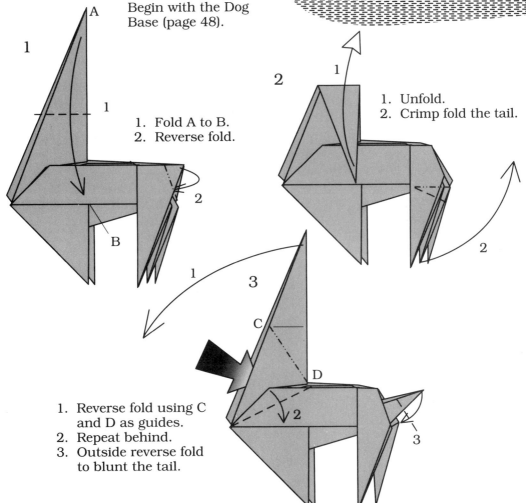

1

1. Fold A to B.
2. Reverse fold.

2

1. Unfold.
2. Crimp fold the tail.

3

1. Reverse fold using C and D as guides.
2. Repeat behind.
3. Outside reverse fold to blunt the tail.

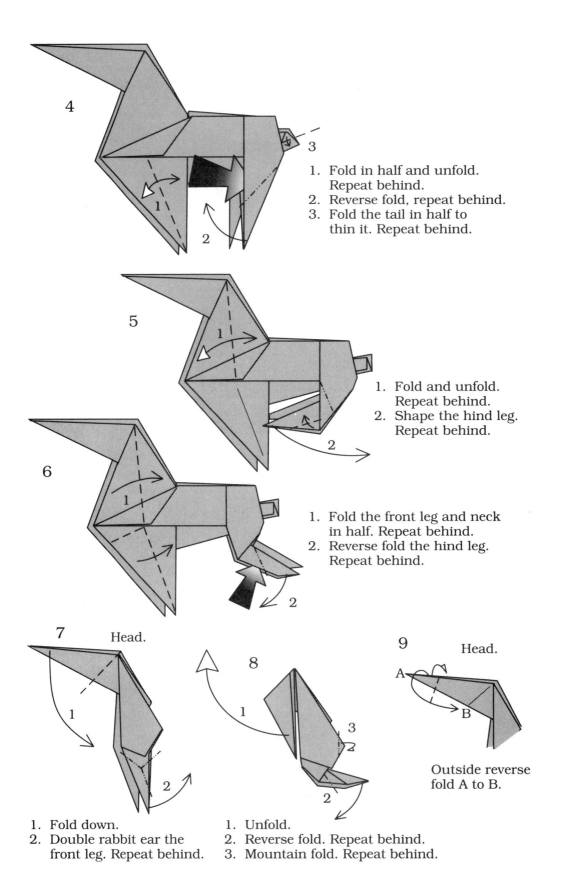

4

3

1. Fold in half and unfold. Repeat behind.
2. Reverse fold, repeat behind.
3. Fold the tail in half to thin it. Repeat behind.

5

1. Fold and unfold. Repeat behind.
2. Shape the hind leg. Repeat behind.

6

1. Fold the front leg and neck in half. Repeat behind.
2. Reverse fold the hind leg. Repeat behind.

7 Head.

1. Fold down.
2. Double rabbit ear the front leg. Repeat behind.

8

1. Unfold.
2. Reverse fold. Repeat behind.
3. Mountain fold. Repeat behind.

9 Head.

A

B

Outside reverse fold A to B.

10

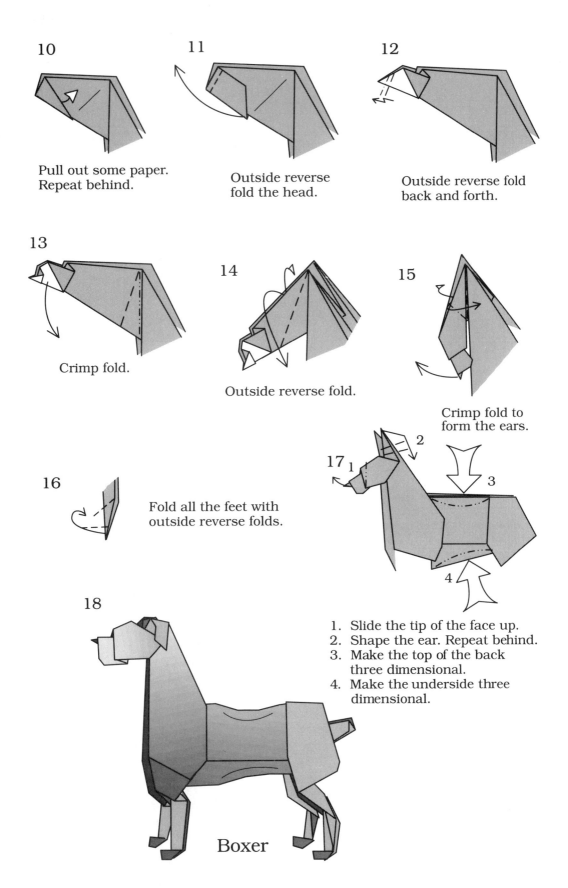

Pull out some paper. Repeat behind.

11

Outside reverse fold the head.

12

Outside reverse fold back and forth.

13

Crimp fold.

14

Outside reverse fold.

15

Crimp fold to form the ears.

16

Fold all the feet with outside reverse folds.

17

1. Slide the tip of the face up.
2. Shape the ear. Repeat behind.
3. Make the top of the back three dimensional.
4. Make the underside three dimensional.

18

Boxer

Scottish Terrier

Also called a scottie, this dog is considered to be the oldest of the Highland terriers. Less than one foot high at the shoulder, this long haired dog is powerful and agile. It weighs about 20 pounds.

Begin with step 23 of the Dog Base (page 48).

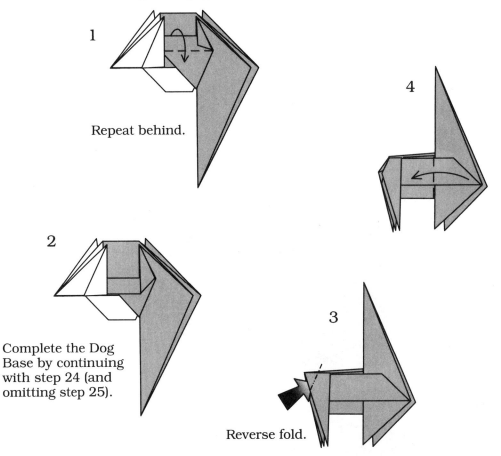

1

Repeat behind.

2

Complete the Dog Base by continuing with step 24 (and omitting step 25).

3

Reverse fold.

4

5

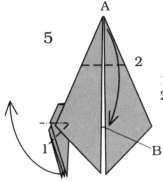

A

2

1. Crimp fold the tail.
2. Fold A to B.

1

B

14

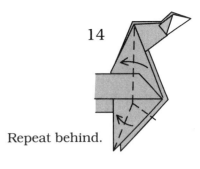

Repeat behind.

6

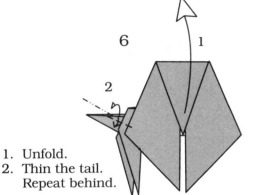

1

2

1. Unfold.
2. Thin the tail.
   Repeat behind.

13

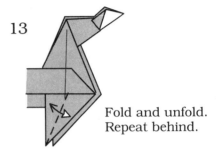

Fold and unfold.
Repeat behind.

7

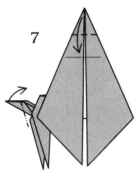

Reverse fold the tail up.

12

Fold and unfold.
Repeat behind.

11

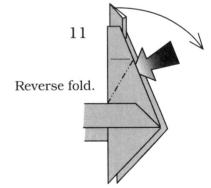

Reverse fold.

Head.

8

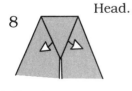

Pull out some paper.

9

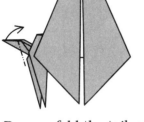

10

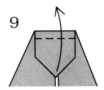

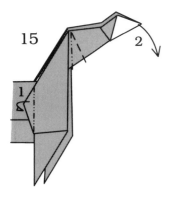

15

1. Repeat behind.
2. Crimp fold the head.

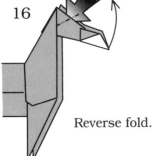

16

Reverse fold.

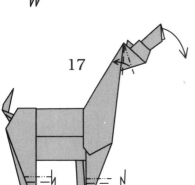

17

Repeat behind.

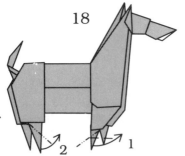

18

1. Crimp fold
2. Reverse fold.
Repeat behind.

22

Scottish Terrier

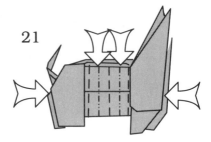

21

Make the body
three dimensional.

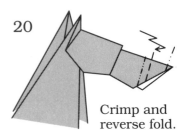

20

Crimp and
reverse fold.

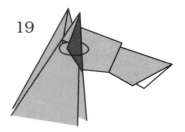

19

Fold the darker grey paper
inside-out. Repeat behind.

58

Dachshund

This is one of the most popular pets because it is obedient, faithful, and intelligent. It is also a good sporting dog, used for hunting animals that live below the ground. This long bodied lively dog with short legs and long ears is usually reddish brown or black and tan. It has a shoulder height of about eight inches and weighs 12–22 pounds.

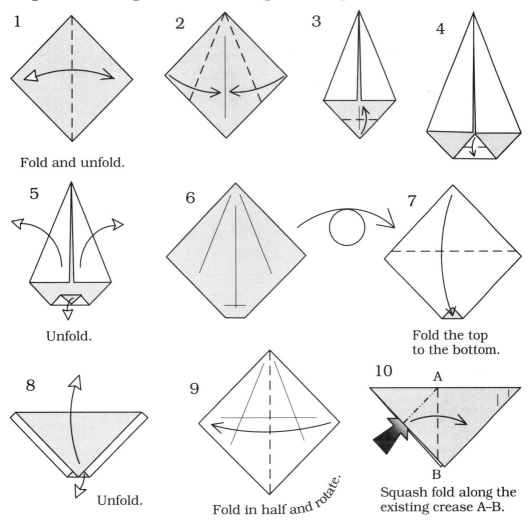

1
Fold and unfold.

2

3

4

5
Unfold.

6

7
Fold the top to the bottom.

8
Unfold.

9
Fold in half and rotate.

10
A

B
Squash fold along the existing crease A–B.

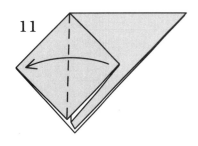

11

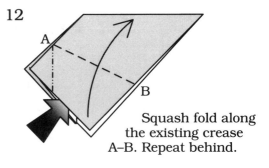

12

Squash fold along
the existing crease
A–B. Repeat behind.

13

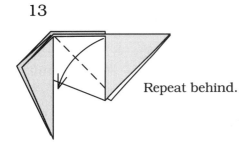

Repeat behind.

14

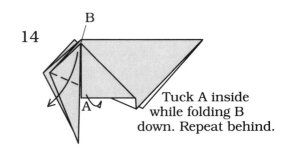

Tuck A inside
while folding B
down. Repeat behind.

15

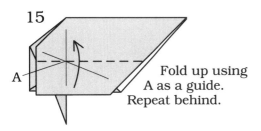

Fold up using
A as a guide.
Repeat behind.

16

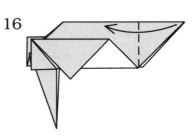

17

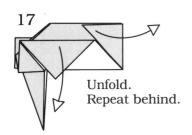

Unfold.
Repeat behind.

18

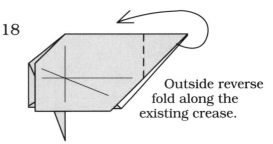

Outside reverse
fold along the
existing crease.

19   A

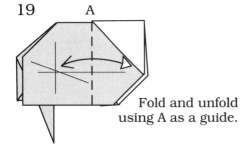

Fold and unfold
using A as a guide.

20

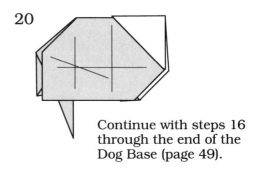

Continue with steps 16
through the end of the
Dog Base (page 49).

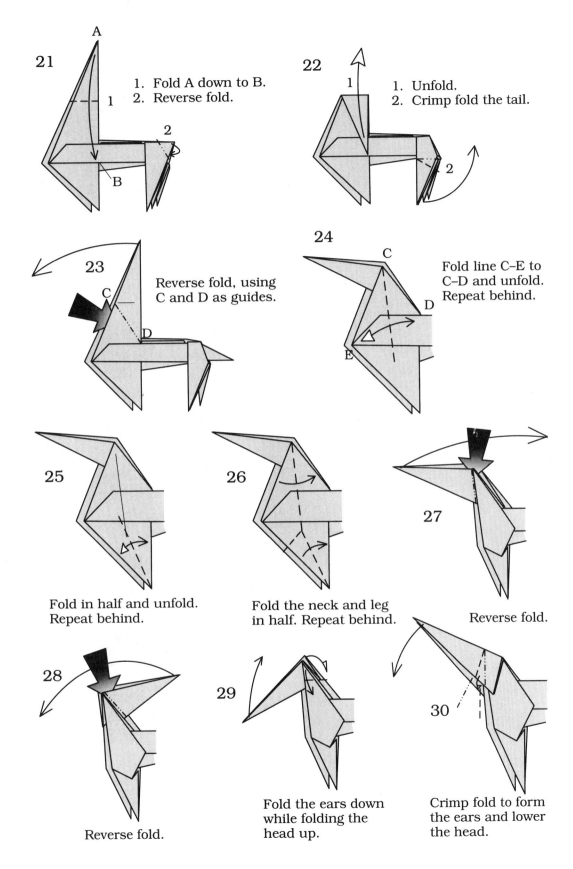

21

A

1. Fold A down to B.
2. Reverse fold.

B

22

1. Unfold.
2. Crimp fold the tail.

23

Reverse fold, using C and D as guides.

C

D

24

C

D

E

Fold line C–E to C–D and unfold. Repeat behind.

25

Fold in half and unfold. Repeat behind.

26

Fold the neck and leg in half. Repeat behind.

27

Reverse fold.

28

Reverse fold.

29

Fold the ears down while folding the head up.

30

Crimp fold to form the ears and lower the head.

DACHSHUND

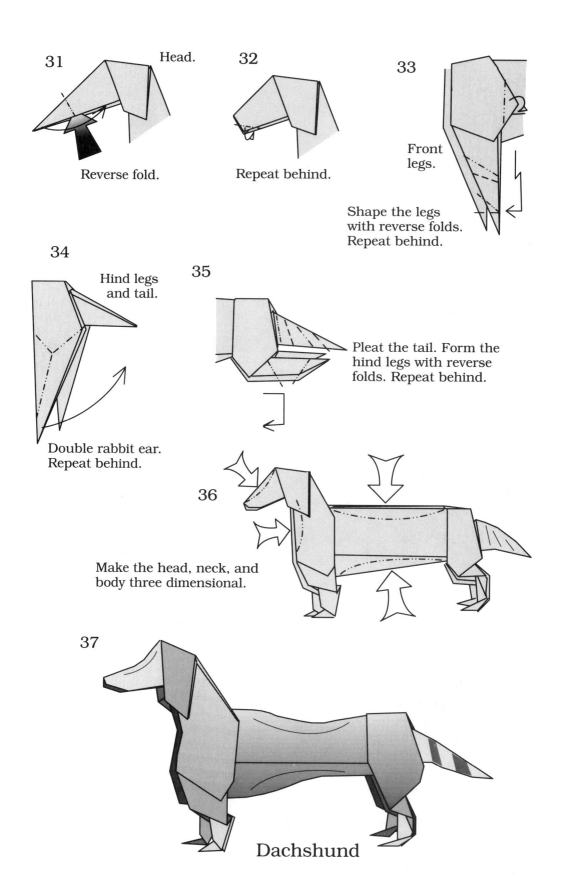

31 Head.

Reverse fold.

32

Repeat behind.

33

Front legs.

Shape the legs with reverse folds. Repeat behind.

34 Hind legs and tail.

35

Pleat the tail. Form the hind legs with reverse folds. Repeat behind.

Double rabbit ear. Repeat behind.

36

Make the head, neck, and body three dimensional.

37

Dachshund

Husky

These mixed-breed working dogs pull sleds. They have helped on more polar journeys than any other dog. Gray or black and white, these affectionate, friendly dogs are about two feet tall at the shoulder.

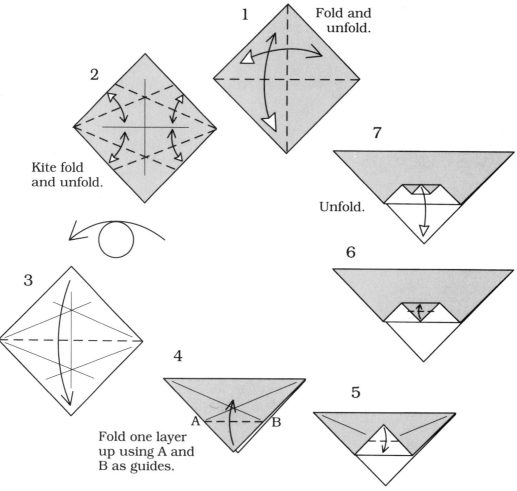

1 Fold and unfold.

2 Kite fold and unfold.

3

4 Fold one layer up using A and B as guides.

A   B

5

6

7 Unfold.

8

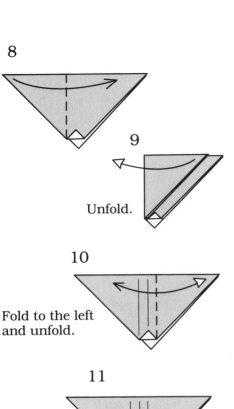

9

Unfold.

10

Fold to the left
and unfold.

11

Unfold.

12

Squash fold.

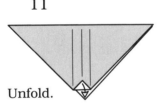

13

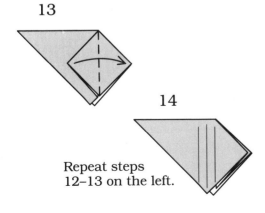

14

Repeat steps
12–13 on the left.

15

Squash fold.

16

Unfold.

17

Repeat steps 15–16 on
the right and back.

18

Fold up and unfold.
Repeat behind.

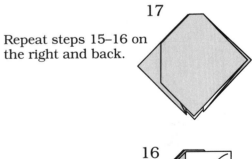

19

Repeat behind.

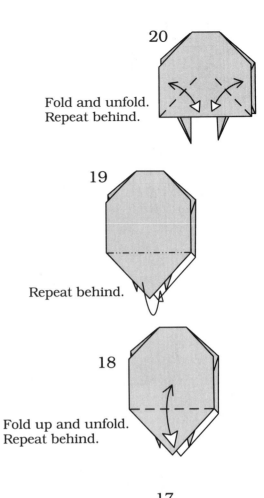

20

Fold and unfold.
Repeat behind.

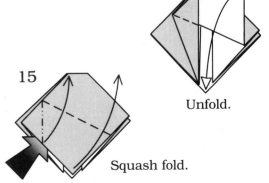

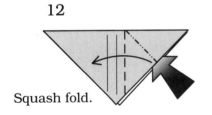

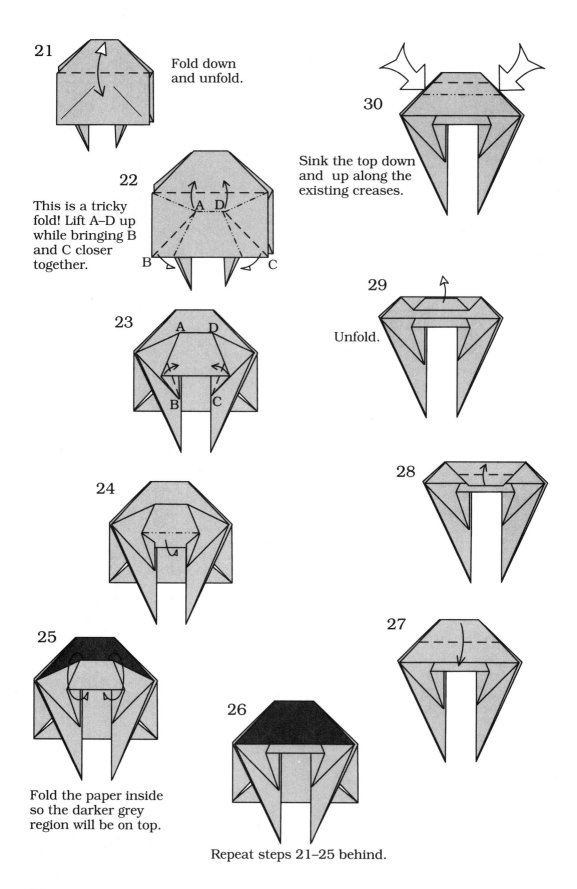

21 Fold down and unfold.

22 This is a tricky fold! Lift A–D up while bringing B and C closer together.

30 Sink the top down and up along the existing creases.

29 Unfold.

23

28

24

27

25 Fold the paper inside so the darker grey region will be on top.

26 Repeat steps 21–25 behind.

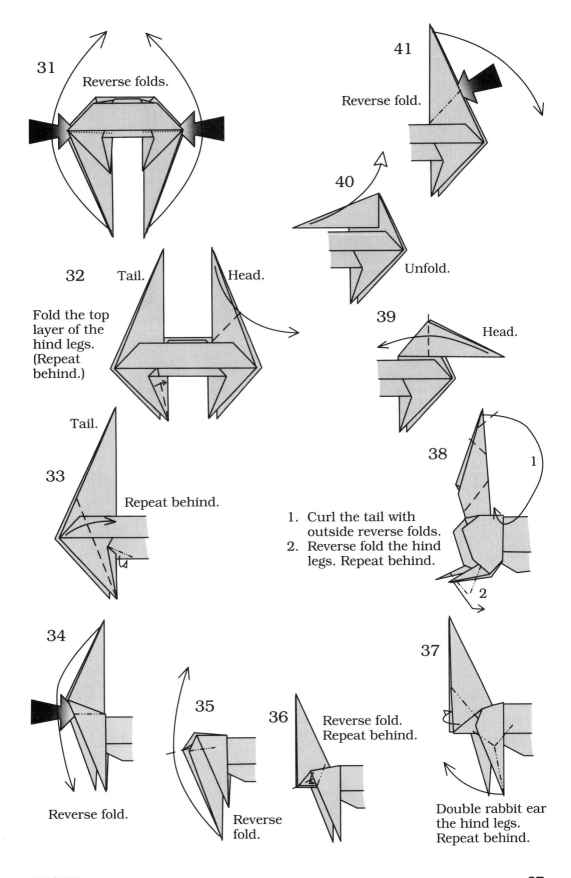

31 Reverse folds.

32 Tail. Head.

Fold the top layer of the hind legs. (Repeat behind.)

33 Tail.

Repeat behind.

34 Reverse fold.

35 Reverse fold.

36 Reverse fold. Repeat behind.

37 Double rabbit ear the hind legs. Repeat behind.

38
1. Curl the tail with outside reverse folds.
2. Reverse fold the hind legs. Repeat behind.

39 Head.

40 Unfold.

41 Reverse fold.

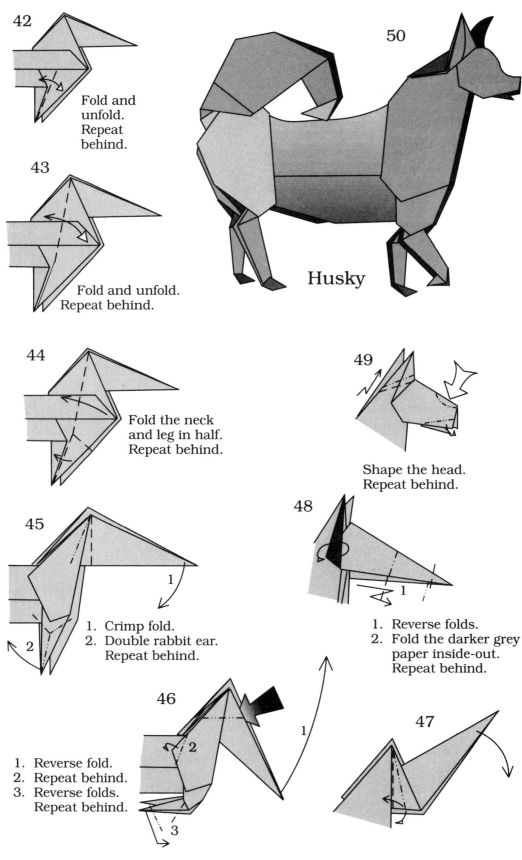

42

Fold and
unfold.
Repeat
behind.

43

Fold and unfold.
Repeat behind.

50

Husky

44

Fold the neck
and leg in half.
Repeat behind.

49

Shape the head.
Repeat behind.

45

1. Crimp fold.
2. Double rabbit ear.
   Repeat behind.

1

2

48

1. Reverse folds.
2. Fold the darker grey
   paper inside-out.
   Repeat behind.

1

46

1. Reverse fold.
2. Repeat behind.
3. Reverse folds.
   Repeat behind.

2

3

1

47

Penguin

This flightless, aquatic bird lives along the coastlines in the southern hemisphere. It is very well adapted to the cold and is an extremely fast swimmer. On land, it can run, hop, or slide on its belly. The adult is from one to four feet tall and weighs from 4 to 90 pounds. Underwater, it eats fish, shrimp, and shellfish. It spends most of its time at sea and only goes on land to breed and molt.

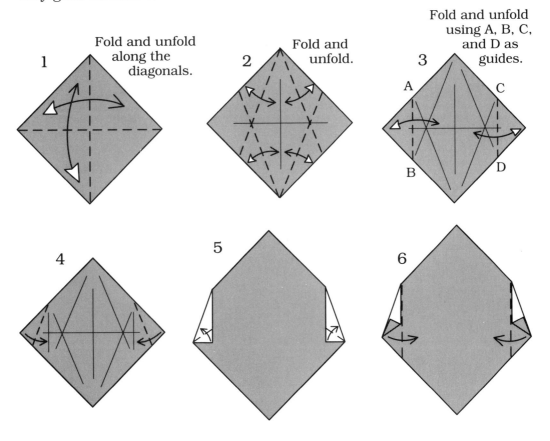

1 Fold and unfold along the diagonals.

2 Fold and unfold.

3 Fold and unfold using A, B, C, and D as guides.

4

5

6

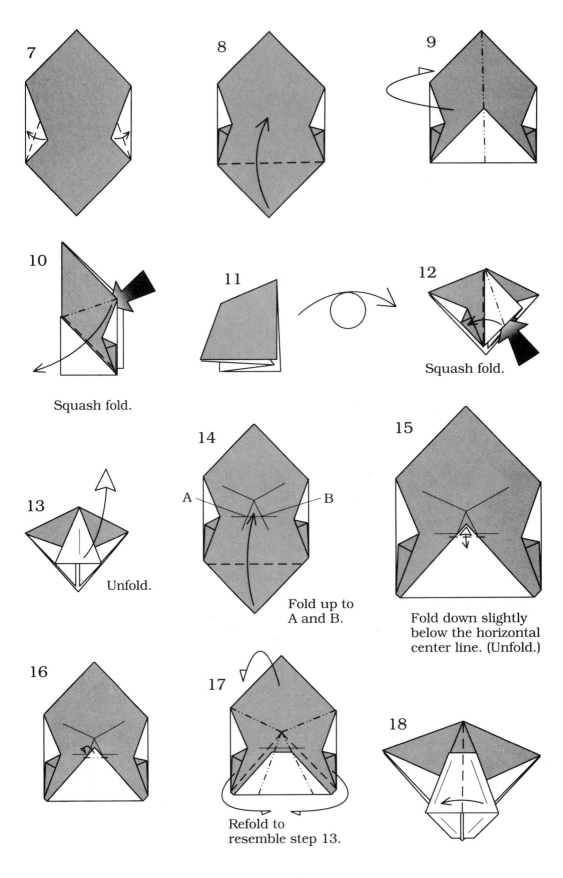

7

8

9

10

Squash fold.

11

12

Squash fold.

13

Unfold.

14

A   B

Fold up to
A and B.

15

Fold down slightly
below the horizontal
center line. (Unfold.)

16

17

Refold to
resemble step 13.

18

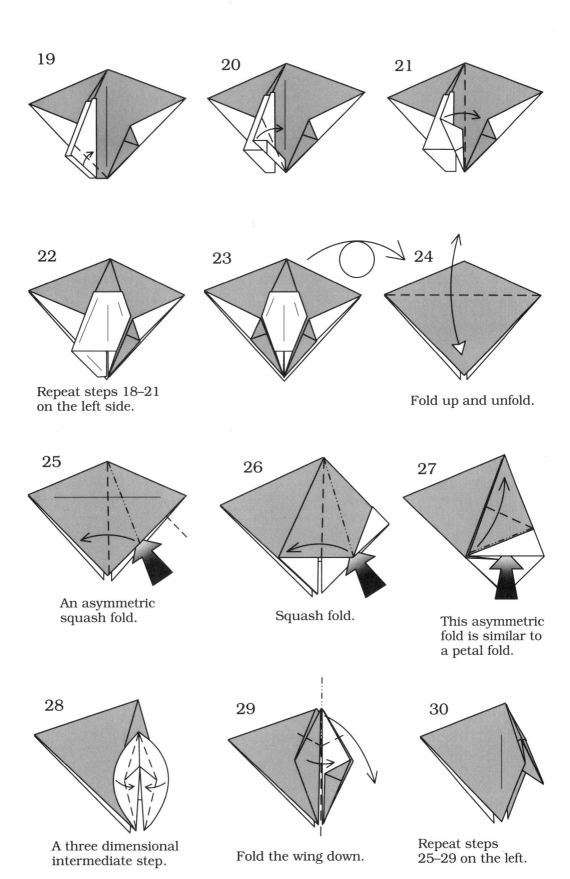

19

20

21

22

Repeat steps 18–21
on the left side.

23

24

Fold up and unfold.

25

An asymmetric
squash fold.

26

Squash fold.

27

This asymmetric
fold is similar to
a petal fold.

28

A three dimensional
intermediate step.

29

Fold the wing down.

30

Repeat steps
25–29 on the left.

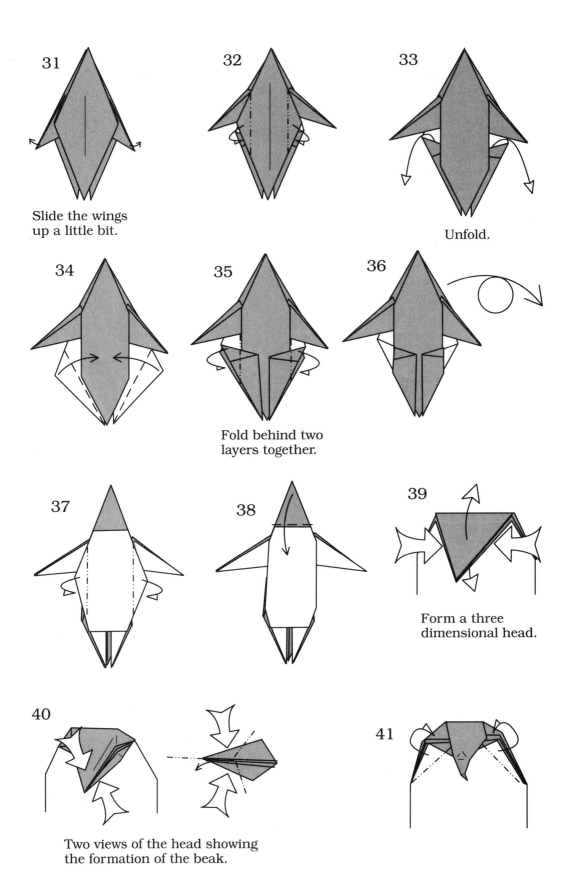

31

Slide the wings
up a little bit.

32

33

Unfold.

34

35

Fold behind two
layers together.

36

37

38

39

Form a three
dimensional head.

40

Two views of the head showing
the formation of the beak.

41

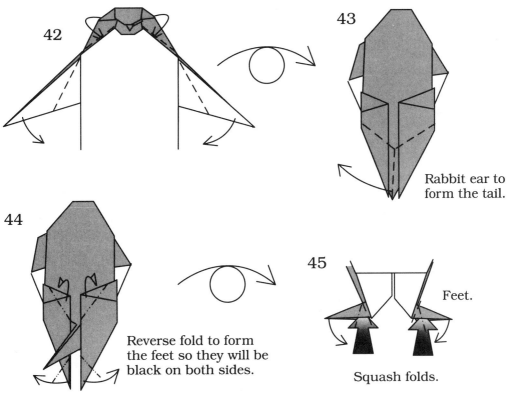

42

43

Rabbit ear to form the tail.

44

Reverse fold to form the feet so they will be black on both sides.

45

Feet.

Squash folds.

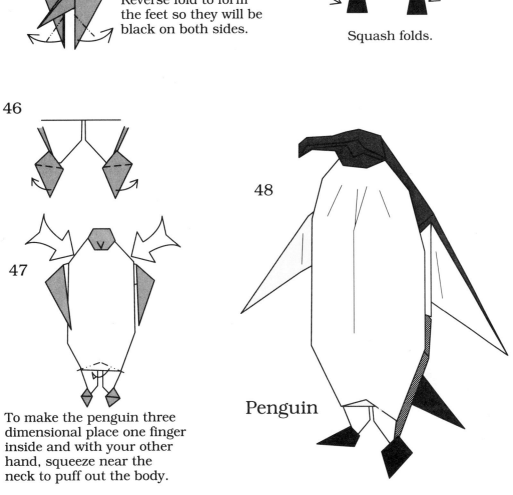

46

47

48

To make the penguin three dimensional place one finger inside and with your other hand, squeeze near the neck to puff out the body.

Penguin

Peacock

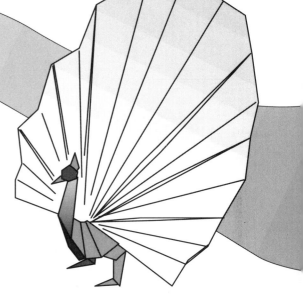

The peacock, which is the male peafowl, has a large green or blue body plumage and head crests. In full plumage it is about seven feet tall. The plumes, which are long features, are not the tail. It lives by river banks, forest clearings, or other places with scattered trees. It flies quite well and travels in small flocks. The peacock feeds on seeds and grasses.

1

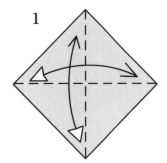

Fold and unfold along the diagonals.

2

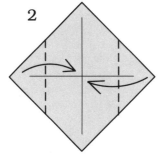

Fold two corners to the center.

3

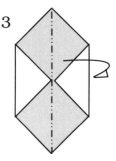

4

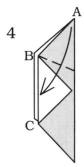

Bring A down to the line B–C.

5

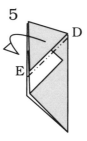

Fold behind along D–E.

6

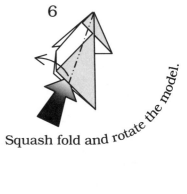

Squash fold and rotate the model.

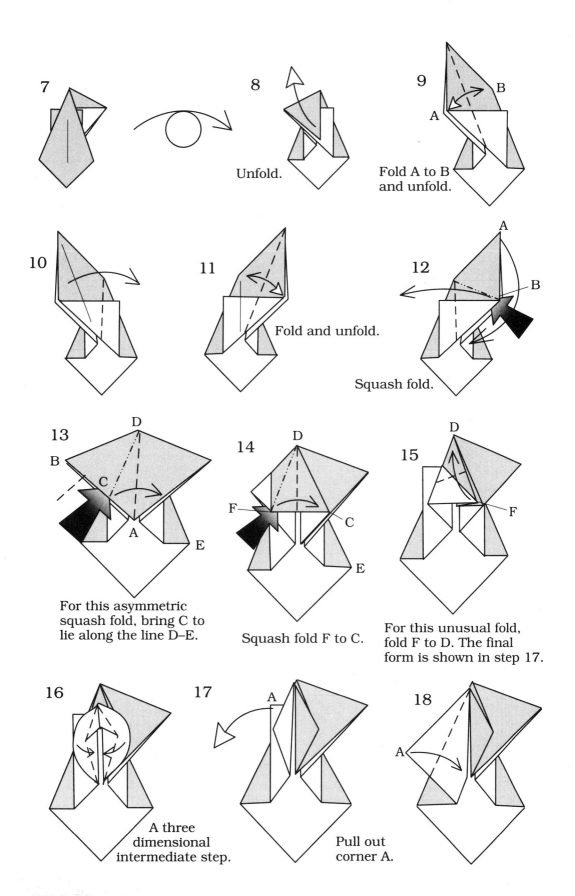

7

8 Unfold.

9 Fold A to B and unfold.

10

11 Fold and unfold.

12 Squash fold.

13 For this asymmetric squash fold, bring C to lie along the line D–E.

14 Squash fold F to C.

15 For this unusual fold, fold F to D. The final form is shown in step 17.

16 A three dimensional intermediate step.

17 Pull out corner A.

18

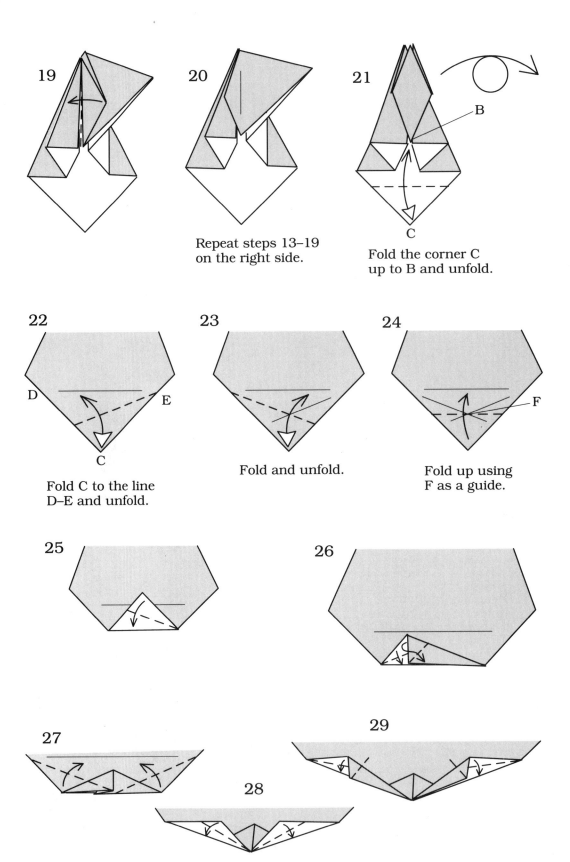

19

20

Repeat steps 13–19
on the right side.

21

B

C

Fold the corner C
up to B and unfold.

22

D

E

C

Fold C to the line
D–E and unfold.

23

Fold and unfold.

24

F

Fold up using
F as a guide.

25

26

27

28

29

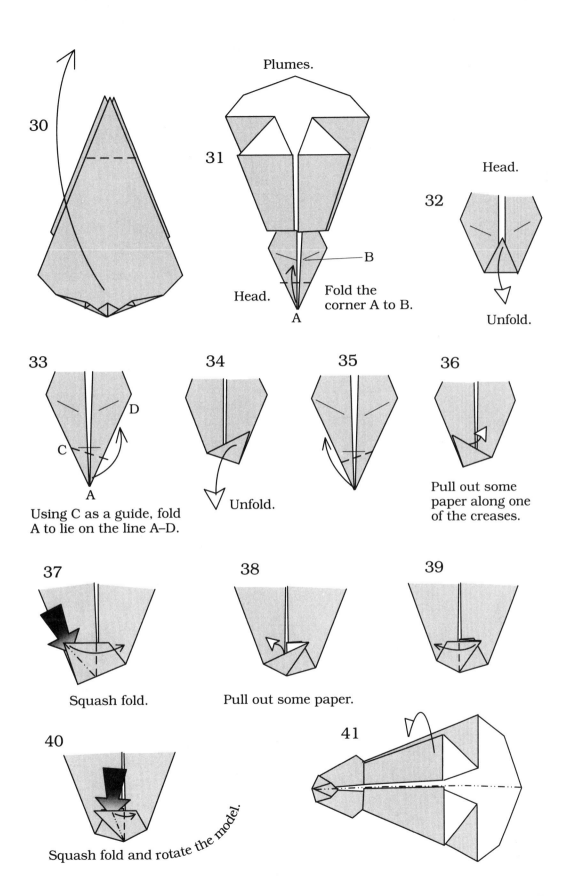

30

31

Plumes.

Head.

Fold the corner A to B.

B

A

Head.

32

Unfold.

33

D

C

A

Using C as a guide, fold A to lie on the line A–D.

34

Unfold.

35

36

Pull out some paper along one of the creases.

37

Squash fold.

38

Pull out some paper.

39

40

Squash fold and rotate the model.

41

42

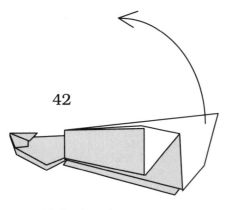

Slide the plumes up.

43

Plumes.

Head.

A

B

Legs and tail.

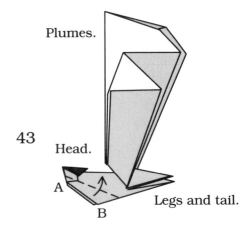

Fold A–B up so that it is under the darker paper. Repeat behind.

44

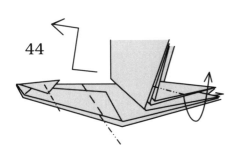

Outside reverse folds form the neck. Lift up some paper by the tail to shape the wings. Repeat behind.

45

1

2

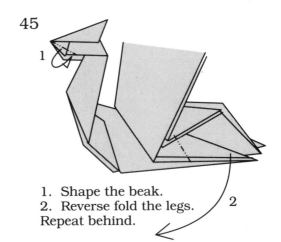

1. Shape the beak.
2. Reverse fold the legs. Repeat behind.

46

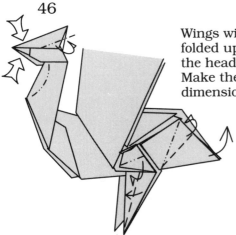

Wings will form as the tail is folded up. Pinch the tip of the head to form the beak. Make the neck three dimensional. Repeat behind.

47

Leg.

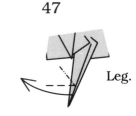

Crimp fold the leg. Repeat behind.

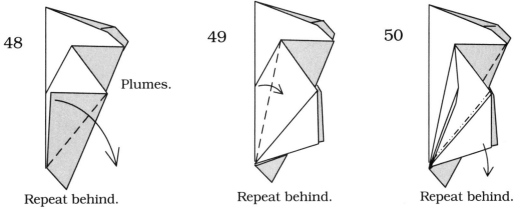

48

Plumes.

Repeat behind.

49

Repeat behind.

50

Repeat behind.

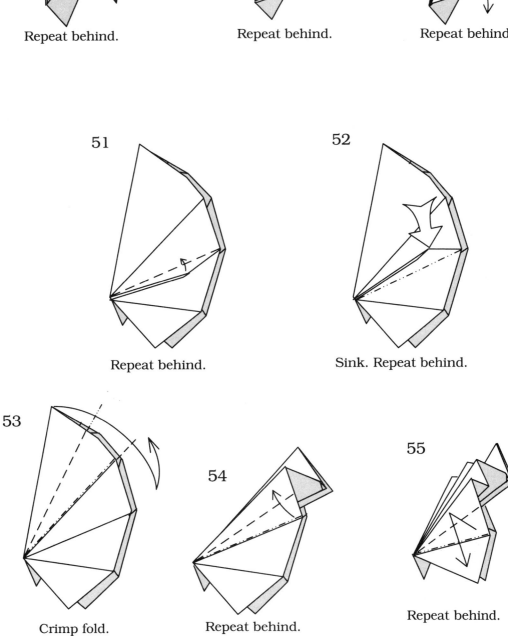

51

Repeat behind.

52

Sink. Repeat behind.

53

Crimp fold.

54

Repeat behind.

55

Repeat behind.

56

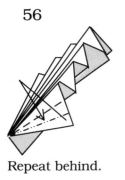

Repeat behind.

57

Unfold. Repeat behind.

58

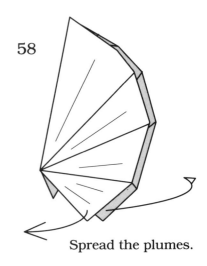

Spread the plumes.

59

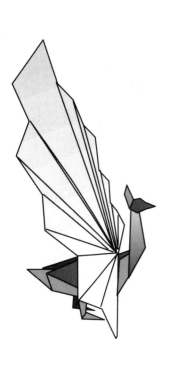

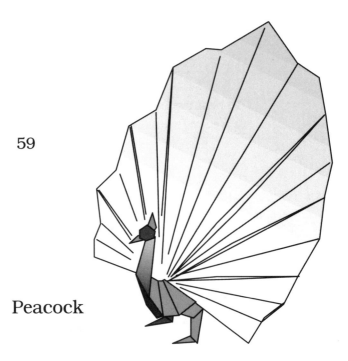

Peacock

Horse

Horses have been associated with mankind throughout history. For thousands of years, they were hunted for food. Then they became domesticated and were used in warfare to pull chariots. Their use in warfare lasted into this century. Today they are used for riding and racing.

About six feet tall, the horse is highly adapted for fast, graceful running. It feeds on grass.

Begin with step 33 of the Dog Base (page 48).

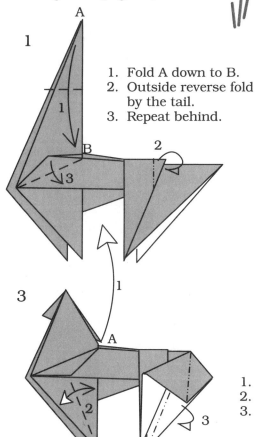

1

A

B

1. Fold A down to B.
2. Outside reverse fold by the tail.
3. Repeat behind.

2

E

B

C

D

1. Squash fold C down to lie on the line C–D.
2. Fold behind along the line E–B.

3

A

1. Unfold — fold A back up.
2. Kite fold and unfold. Repeat behind.
3. Fold behind to shape the tail.

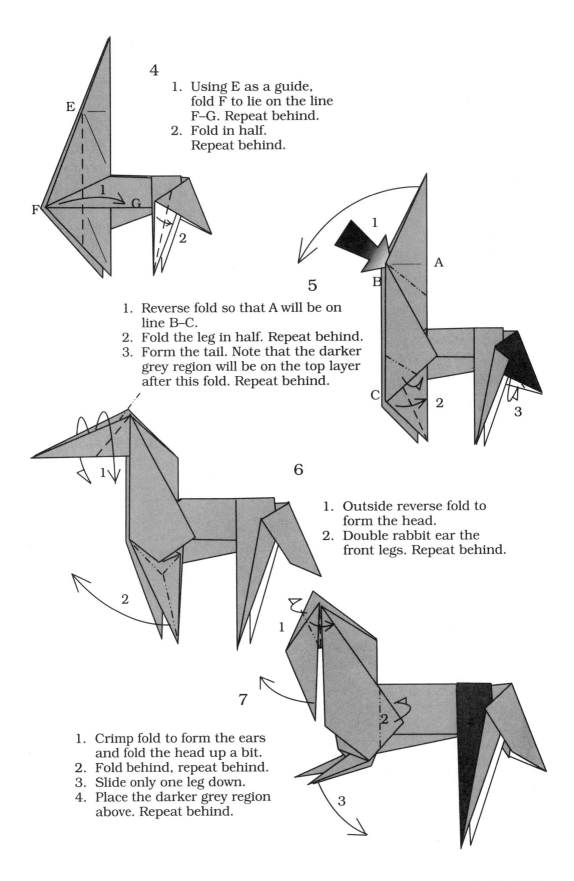

4

1. Using E as a guide, fold F to lie on the line F–G. Repeat behind.
2. Fold in half. Repeat behind.

5

1. Reverse fold so that A will be on line B–C.
2. Fold the leg in half. Repeat behind.
3. Form the tail. Note that the darker grey region will be on the top layer after this fold. Repeat behind.

6

1. Outside reverse fold to form the head.
2. Double rabbit ear the front legs. Repeat behind.

7

1. Crimp fold to form the ears and fold the head up a bit.
2. Fold behind, repeat behind.
3. Slide only one leg down.
4. Place the darker grey region above. Repeat behind.

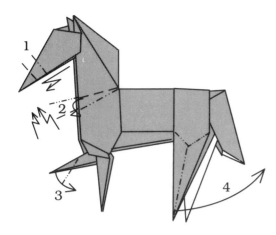

8

1. Crimp fold to form the mouth.
2. Crimp fold to bend the neck.
3. Reverse fold the front leg.
4. Double rabbit ear the hind leg. Repeat behind.

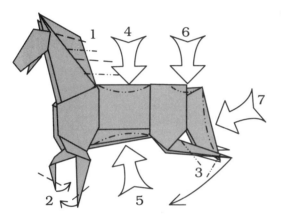

9

1. Pleat the main.
2. Form the front hooves.
3. Shape the hind legs and hooves.
4. Make the back three dimensional.
5. Make the underside three dimensional.
6. Shape the top of the tail.
7. Shape the tail.

10

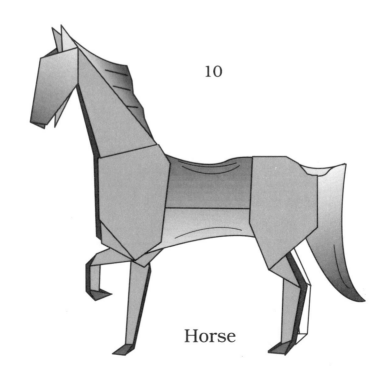

Horse

Bison

The American bison used to live in the Great Plains of North America. Indians hunted bison for food and clothing. Today bison are mainly found in game reserves. They are about eleven feet long and six feet high at the shoulder, and they weigh about a ton. Primarily grazers, they live in herds. They have a good sense of hearing and smell.

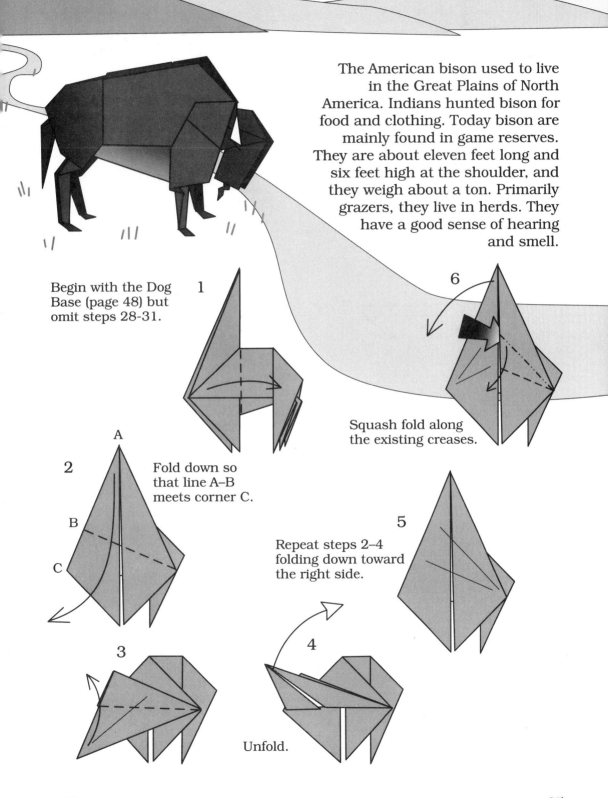

Begin with the Dog Base (page 48) but omit steps 28-31.

1

6

Squash fold along the existing creases.

2

A

B

C

Fold down so that line A–B meets corner C.

5

Repeat steps 2–4 folding down toward the right side.

3

4

Unfold.

7

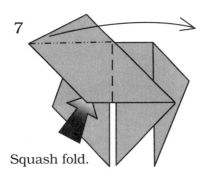

Squash fold.

8

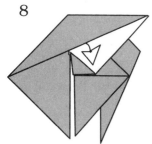

Pull out
some paper.

9

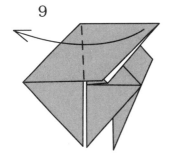

10

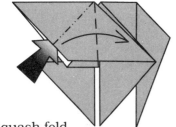

Squash fold.

11

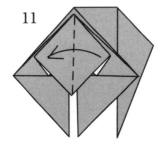

12

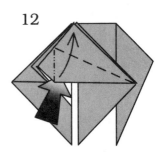

Squash fold.

13

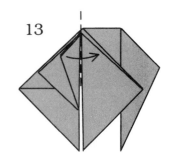

14

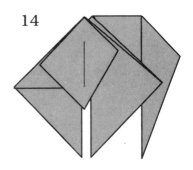

Repeat steps 11–13
on the left side.

15

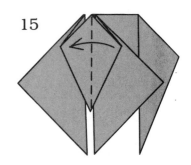

ORIGAMI SCULPTURES

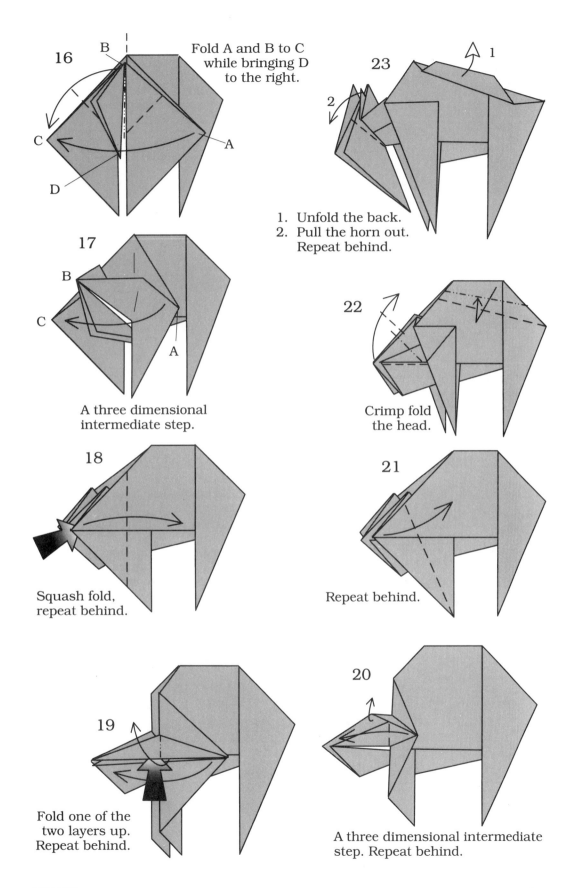

16 B

Fold A and B to C
while bringing D
to the right.

C

A

D

23

1

2

1. Unfold the back.
2. Pull the horn out.
   Repeat behind.

17

B

C

A

A three dimensional
intermediate step.

22

Crimp fold
the head.

18

Squash fold,
repeat behind.

21

Repeat behind.

19

Fold one of the
two layers up.
Repeat behind.

20

A three dimensional intermediate
step. Repeat behind.

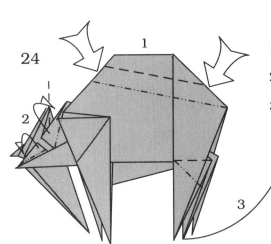

24

1. Sink down and up to form the back.
2. Reverse folds at the head. Repeat behind.
3. Crimp fold the tail.

25

1. Reverse fold the tip of the head inside.
2. Fold the horn to the right. Repeat behind.
3. Crimp fold the beard.
4. Crimp fold the front legs. Repeat behind.
5. Double rabbit ear the hind legs. Repeat behind.
6. Thin the tail. Repeat behind.

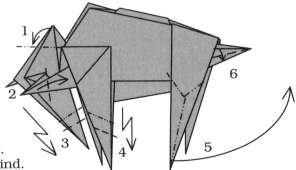

26

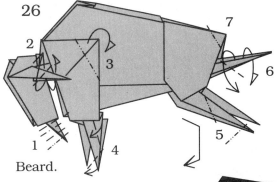

Beard.

1. Pleat the beard.
2. Outside reverse fold the horn up to make it white. Repeat behind.
3. Repeat behind.
4. Shape the front legs. Repeat behind for each leg.
5. Reverse folds to shape the hind legs. Repeat behind.
6. Outside reverse fold the tail.
7. Reverse fold.

27

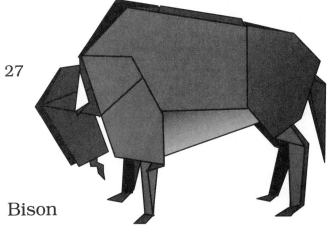

Bison

Camel

This is the two-humped, or Bacterian camel. It is easily tamed and moves slowly. It is seven feet high at the humps and eats salty plants, fish, animal flesh, skin, and bones. Native to the plains of Central Asia, it is well adapted to tolerate cold and snowy winters. Its long, shaggy hair keeps it warm in winter. The camel sheds its coat in the summer.

Begin with the Dog Base (page 48) but omit steps 24-28.

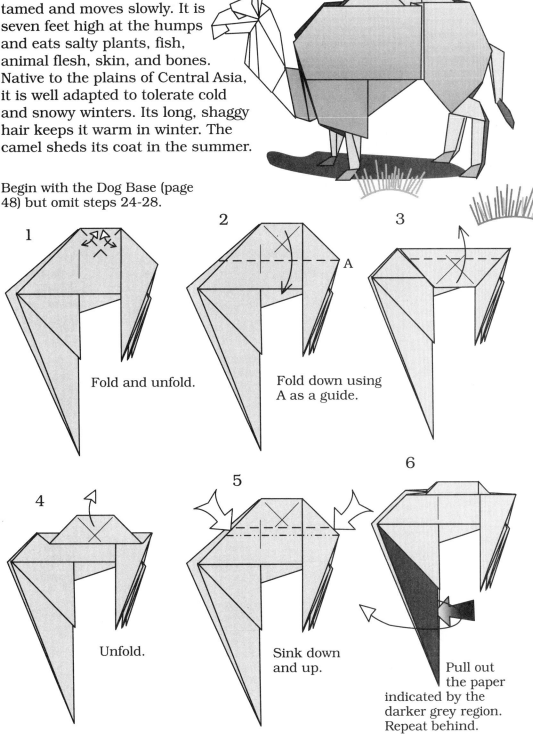

1

Fold and unfold.

2

Fold down using A as a guide.

A

3

4

Unfold.

5

Sink down and up.

6

Pull out the paper indicated by the darker grey region. Repeat behind.

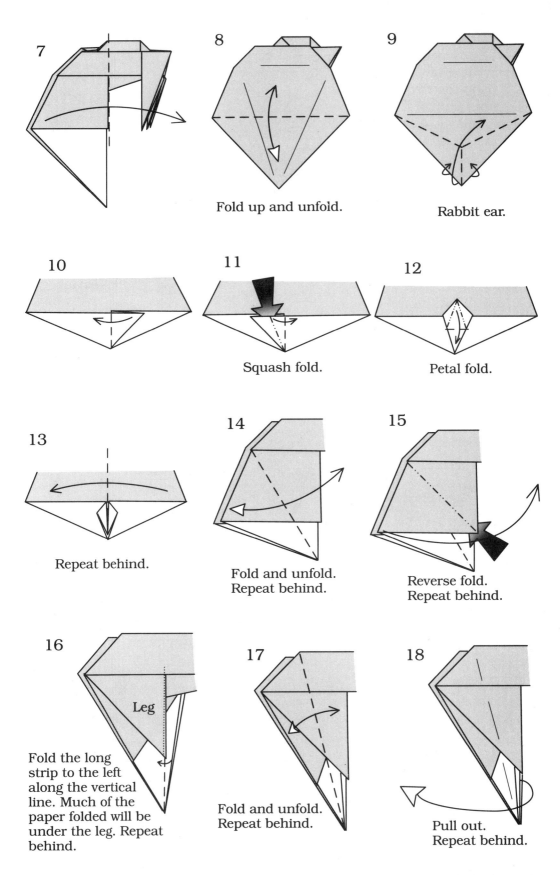

7

8

Fold up and unfold.

9

Rabbit ear.

10

11

Squash fold.

12

Petal fold.

13

Repeat behind.

14

Fold and unfold.
Repeat behind.

15

Reverse fold.
Repeat behind.

16

Leg

Fold the long
strip to the left
along the vertical
line. Much of the
paper folded will be
under the leg. Repeat
behind.

17

Fold and unfold.
Repeat behind.

18

Pull out.
Repeat behind.

19

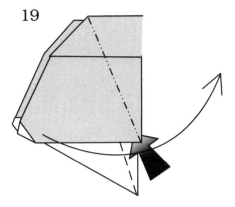

Reverse fold. Repeat behind.

20

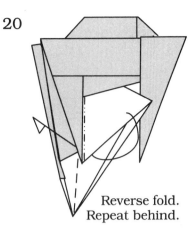

Reverse fold.
Repeat behind.

21

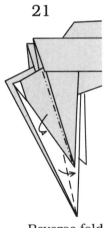

Reverse fold.
Repeat behind.

22

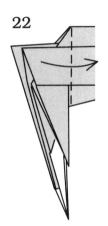

23

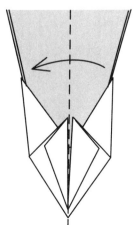

Head.

Pull out the hidden
white paper.

24

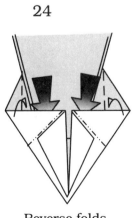

Reverse folds.

25

26

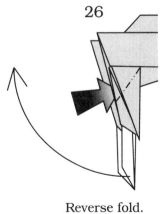

Reverse fold.

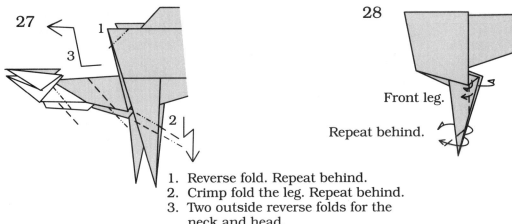

27

1. Reverse fold. Repeat behind.
2. Crimp fold the leg. Repeat behind.
3. Two outside reverse folds for the neck and head.

28

Front leg.

Repeat behind.

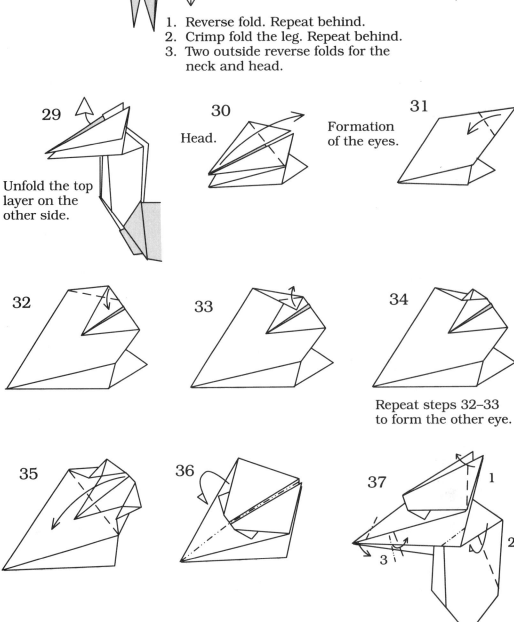

29

Unfold the top layer on the other side.

30

Head.

31

Formation of the eyes.

32

33

34

Repeat steps 32–33 to form the other eye.

35

36

37

1. Fold the ear. Repeat behind.
2. Form the neck. Repeat behind.
3. Crimp fold the mouth.

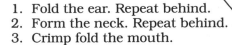

ORIGAMI SCULPTURES

38

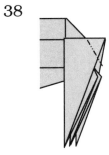

Reverse fold.

39

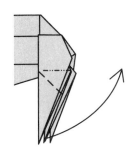

Crimp fold to form the tail.

40

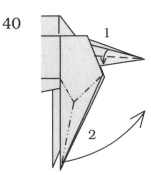

1. Thin the tail.
2. Double rabbit ear to form the hind leg.
Repeat behind.

41

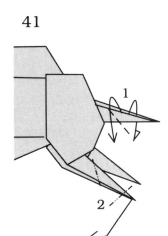

42

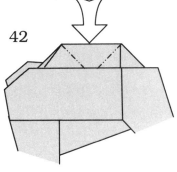

Formation of the humps.

43

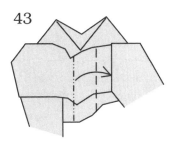

This is a three dimensional figure. Repeat behind.

1. Outside reverse fold the tail.
2. Reverse folds to form the leg and hoof. Repeat behind.

44

45

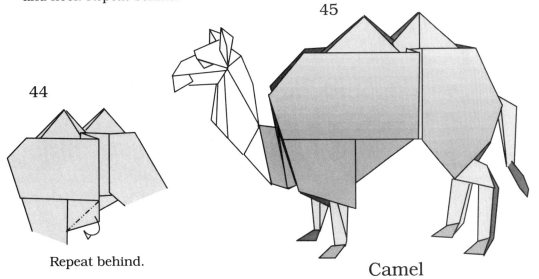

Repeat behind.

Camel

Dromedary

The dromedary, or Arabian camel, has one hump and is completely domesticated. It is seven or eight feet tall at the shoulder and lives in the sandy regions of Western Asia, India, Arabia, and Africa. It is very well adapted to desert life. It has a double layer of protective eyelashes and can shut its nostrils during sand storms. The hump protects it from the sun by absorbing heat and carries its fat reserves. It feeds on plants and can go for three to nine days without water. It has keen eyesight and a good sense of smell.

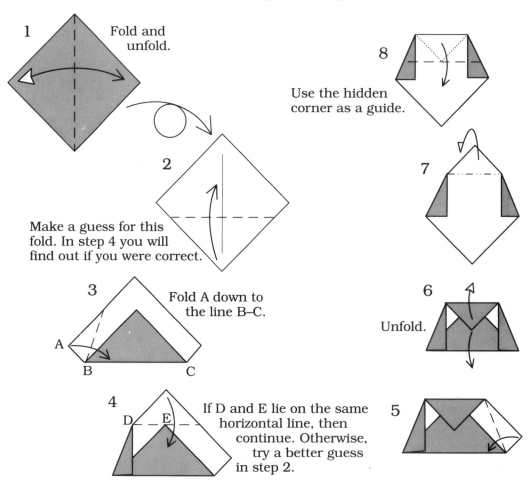

1 Fold and unfold.

2 Make a guess for this fold. In step 4 you will find out if you were correct.

3 Fold A down to the line B–C.
A
B   C

4 If D and E lie on the same horizontal line, then continue. Otherwise, try a better guess in step 2.
D   E

5

6 Unfold.

7

8 Use the hidden corner as a guide.

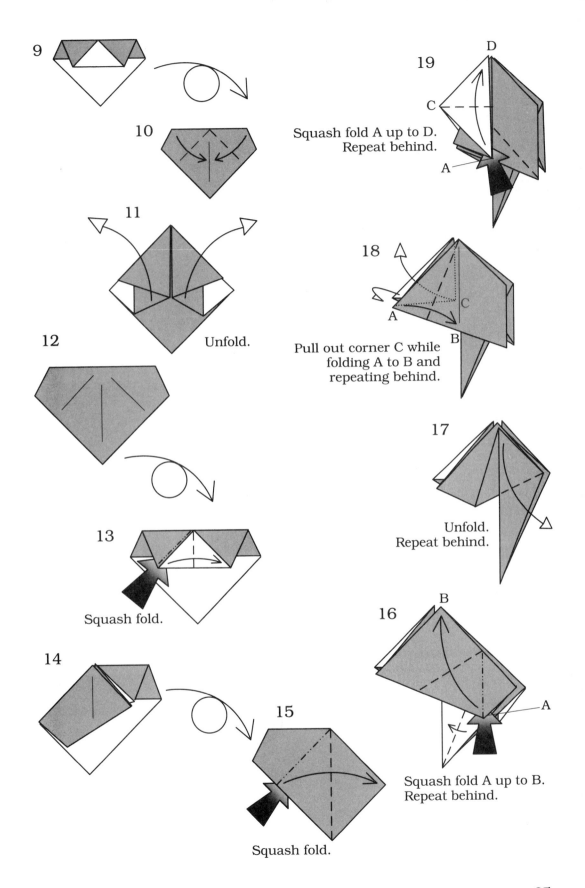

9

10

11

Unfold.

12

13

Squash fold.

14

15

Squash fold.

19

Squash fold A up to D.
Repeat behind.

18

Pull out corner C while
folding A to B and
repeating behind.

17

Unfold.
Repeat behind.

16

Squash fold A up to B.
Repeat behind.

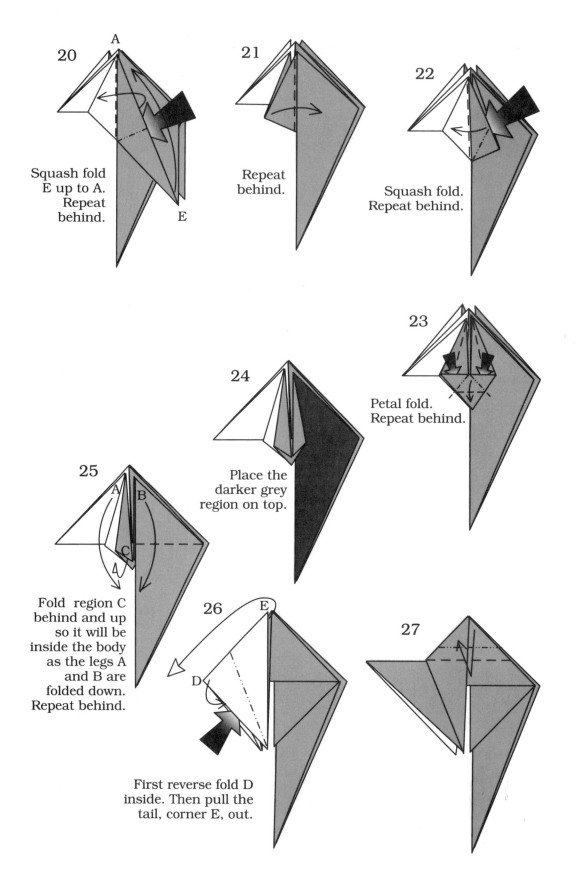

20 Squash fold E up to A. Repeat behind.

21 Repeat behind.

22 Squash fold. Repeat behind.

23 Petal fold. Repeat behind.

24 Place the darker grey region on top.

25 Fold region C behind and up so it will be inside the body as the legs A and B are folded down. Repeat behind.

26 First reverse fold D inside. Then pull the tail, corner E, out.

27

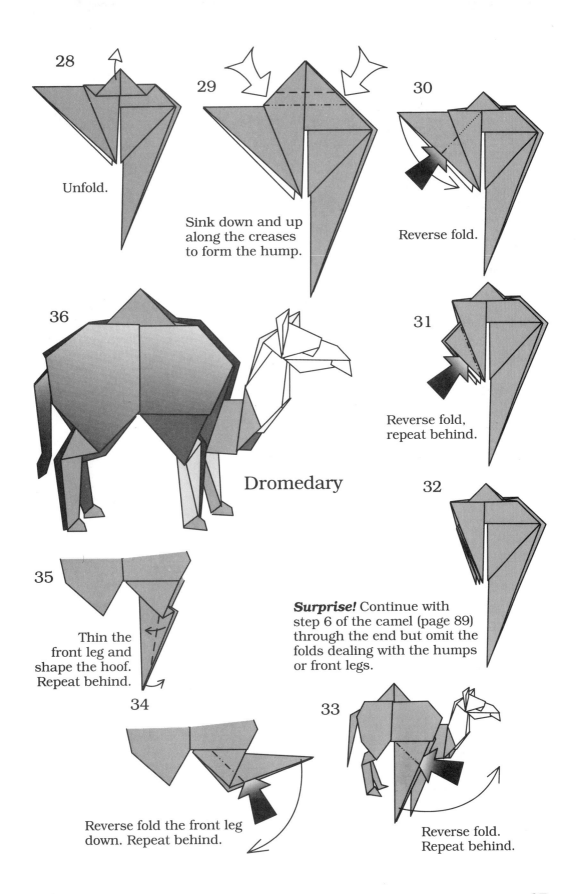

28

Unfold.

29

Sink down and up along the creases to form the hump.

30

Reverse fold.

31

Reverse fold, repeat behind.

36

Dromedary

32

Surprise! Continue with step 6 of the camel (page 89) through the end but omit the folds dealing with the humps or front legs.

35

Thin the front leg and shape the hoof. Repeat behind.

34

Reverse fold the front leg down. Repeat behind.

33

Reverse fold. Repeat behind.

Rhinoceros

This nocturnal mammal lives in the warmer parts of Southern Asia and Africa. It has one or two horns which are made from hardened hairs. During its life, the horns continue to grow and are rubbed down from contact with trees or rocks. Rhinos are good swimmers. The rhinoceros shown here is the white rhinoceros, the largest of the rhinos, standing over six feet high at the shoulder and weighing over three tons. Its pale gray skin sometimes becomes a reddish brown from wallowing in mud. The rhino feeds on grasses and other forms of vegetation.

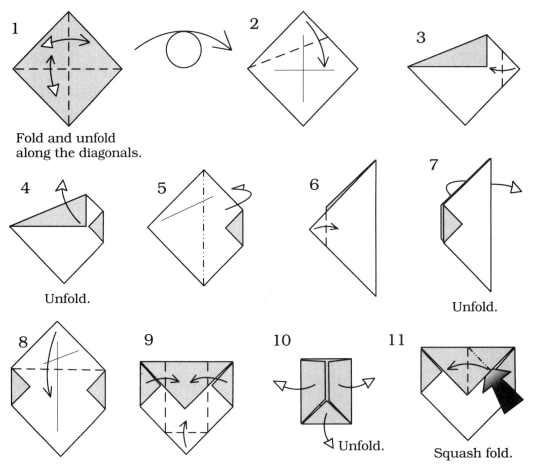

1

Fold and unfold along the diagonals.

2

3

4

Unfold.

5

6

7

Unfold.

8

9

10

Unfold.

11

Squash fold.

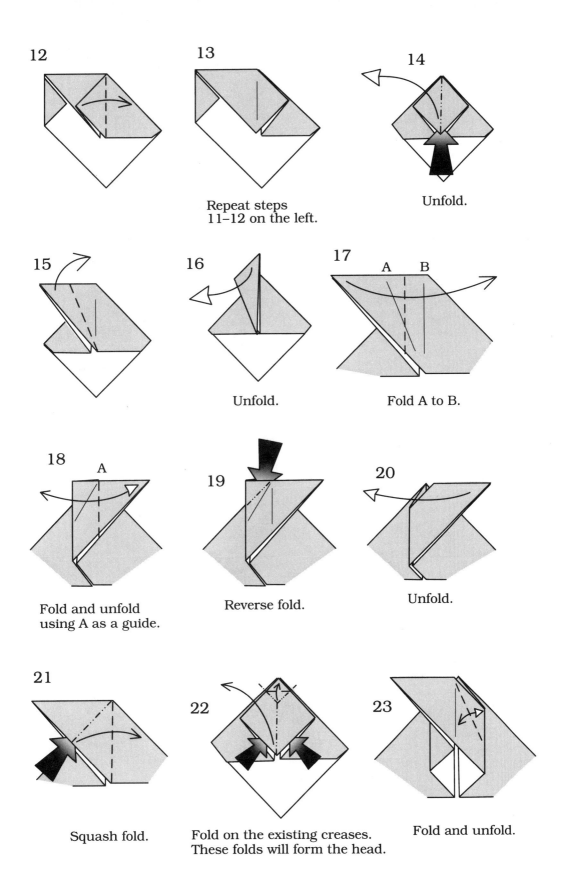

12

13

Repeat steps
11–12 on the left.

14

Unfold.

15

16

Unfold.

17

A B

Fold A to B.

18

A

Fold and unfold
using A as a guide.

19

Reverse fold.

20

Unfold.

21

Squash fold.

22

Fold on the existing creases.
These folds will form the head.

23

Fold and unfold.

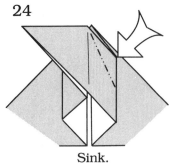

24

Sink.

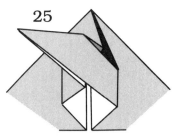

25

This is a three dimensional figure showing the formation of the sink fold.

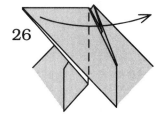

26

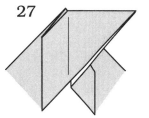

27

Repeat steps 23–24 on the left.

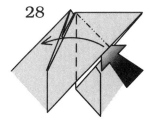

28

Squash fold.

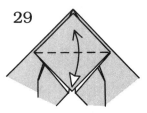

29

Fold up and unfold.

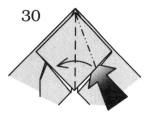

30

Squash fold.

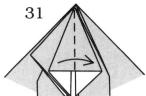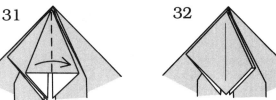

31

32

Repeat steps 30–31 on the left.

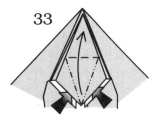

33

Petal fold.

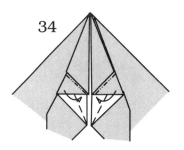

34

Reverse folds.

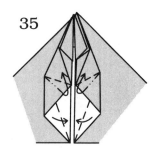

35

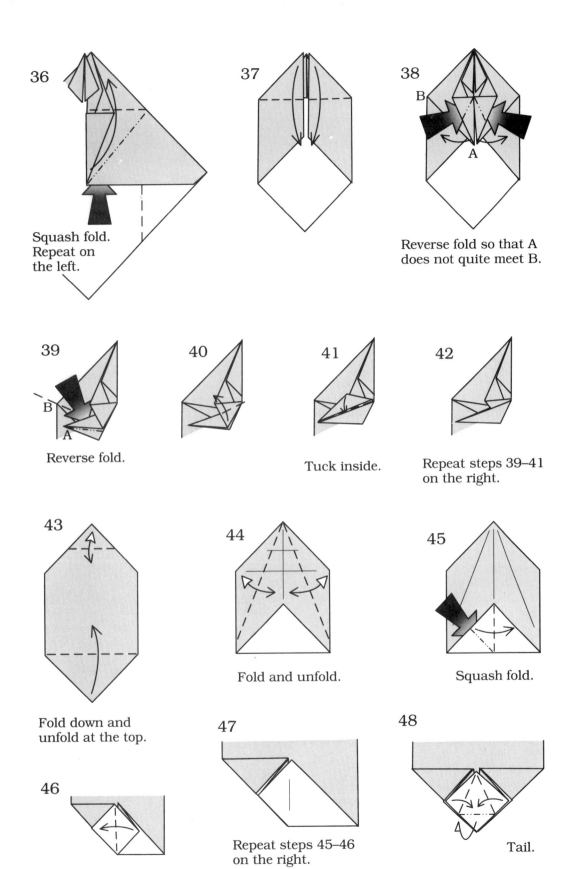

36

Squash fold.
Repeat on
the left.

37

38

B

A

Reverse fold so that A
does not quite meet B.

39

B

A

Reverse fold.

40

41

Tuck inside.

42

Repeat steps 39–41
on the right.

43

Fold down and
unfold at the top.

44

Fold and unfold.

45

Squash fold.

46

47

Repeat steps 45–46
on the right.

48

Tail.

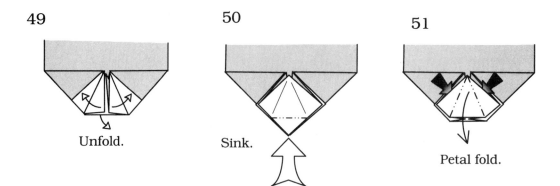

49

Unfold.

50

Sink.

51

Petal fold.

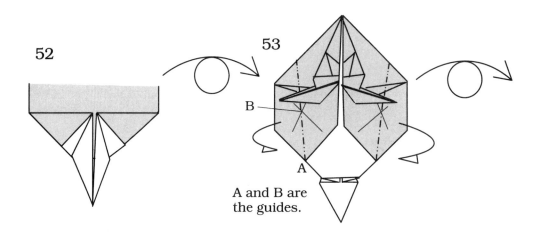

52

53

B

A

A and B are the guides.

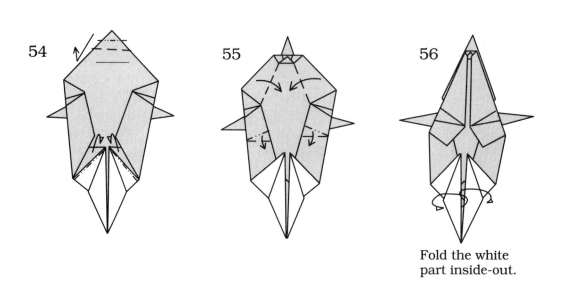

54

55

56

Fold the white part inside-out.

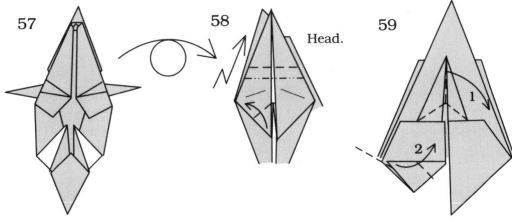

57

58 Head.

59

1. Rabbit ear the horn.
2. Squash fold the ear.

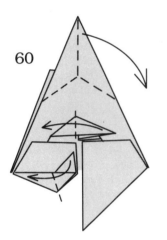

60

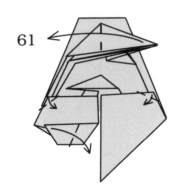

61

Form the other ear
(from steps 58–61).

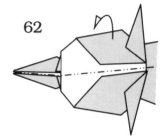

62

Though the body
is folded in half,
do not try to fold
the head in half.

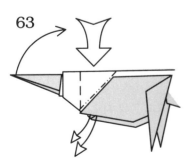

63

Pull out the hind legs
while folding the tail up.

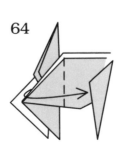

64

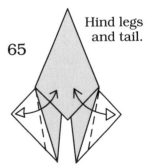

65 Hind legs
and tail.

Fold and unfold.
Note that this crease
does not come to a
point at the bottom.

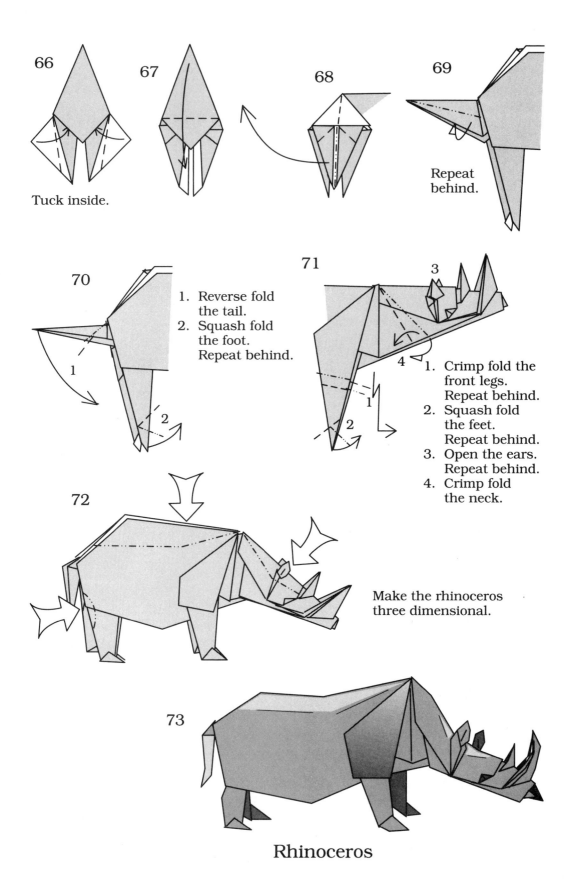

66

Tuck inside.

67

68

69

Repeat behind.

70

1. Reverse fold the tail.
2. Squash fold the foot. Repeat behind.

1

2

71

3

4

1

2

1. Crimp fold the front legs. Repeat behind.
2. Squash fold the feet. Repeat behind.
3. Open the ears. Repeat behind.
4. Crimp fold the neck.

72

Make the rhinoceros three dimensional.

73

Rhinoceros

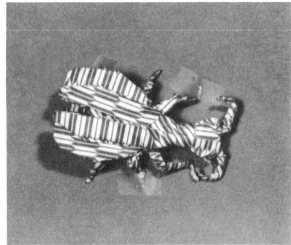

Montroll's Insect Base

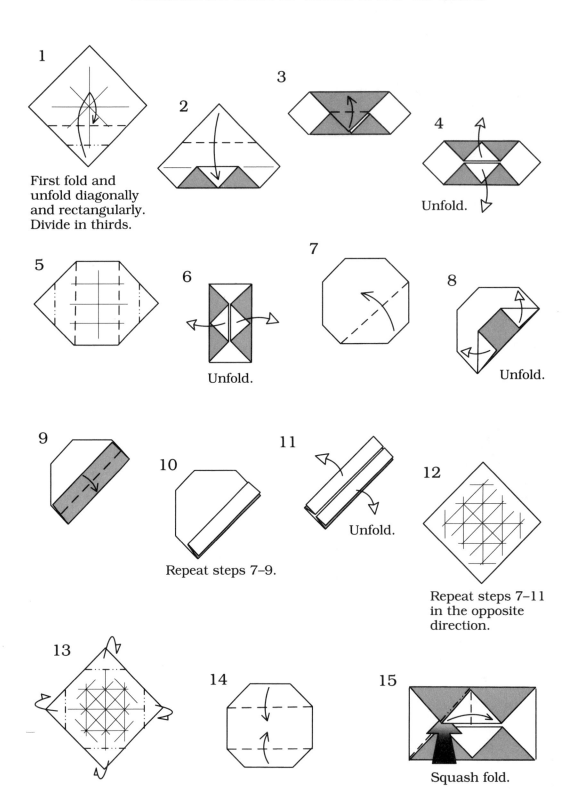

1

First fold and
unfold diagonally
and rectangularly.
Divide in thirds.

2

3

4

Unfold.

5

6

Unfold.

7

8

Unfold.

9

10

Repeat steps 7–9.

11

Unfold.

12

Repeat steps 7–11
in the opposite
direction.

13

14

15

Squash fold.

16

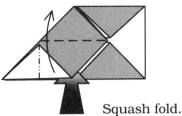

Squash fold.

17

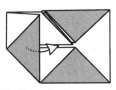

Pull out some paper.

18

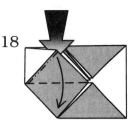

Squash fold.

19

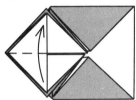

20

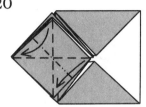

This fold is very similar to the construction of the waterbomb base.

21

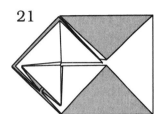

Repeat steps 19–20 on the upper left hand side.

22

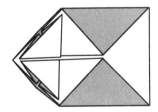

Repeat steps 15–21 on the right.

23

24

25

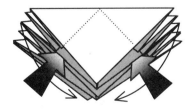

Reverse fold the center flaps down.

Make eight reverse folds. (Four in front and four behind.)

26

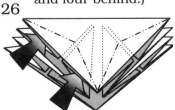

27

Unfold, repeat behind.

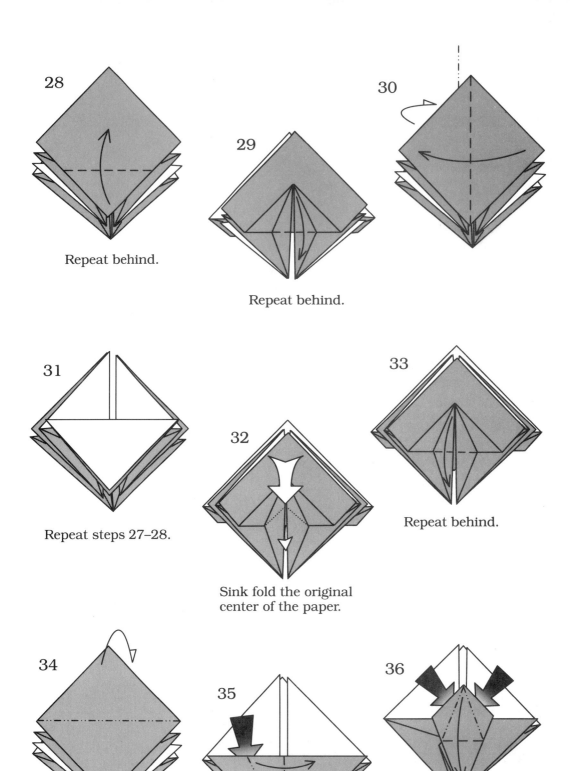

28

Repeat behind.

29

Repeat behind.

30

31

Repeat steps 27–28.

32

Sink fold the original center of the paper.

33

Repeat behind.

34

35

Squash fold.

36

This is similar to a petal fold.

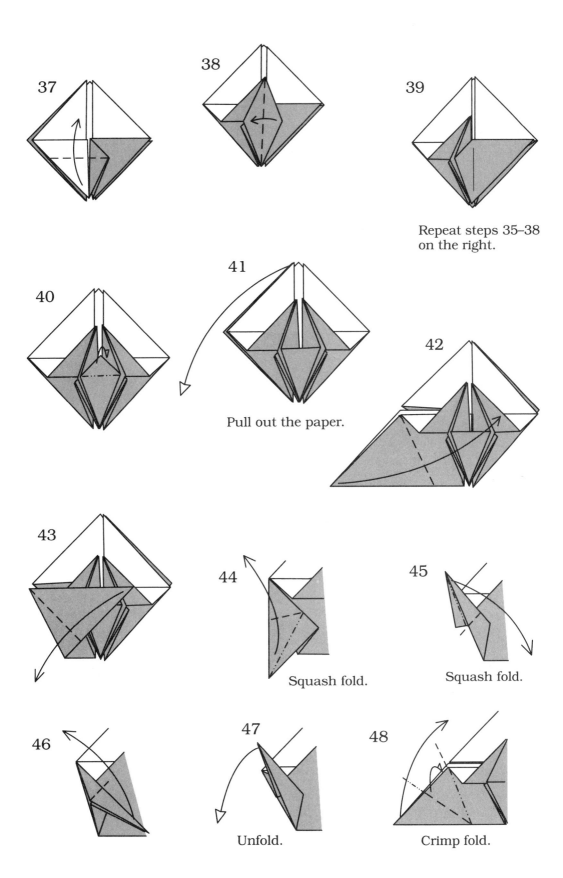

37

38

39

Repeat steps 35–38 on the right.

40

41

Pull out the paper.

42

43

44

Squash fold.

45

Squash fold.

46

47

Unfold.

48

Crimp fold.

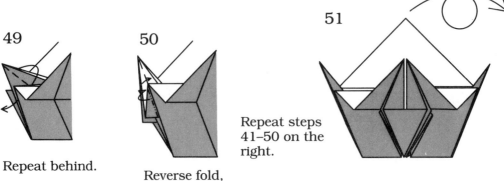

49

Repeat behind.

50

Reverse fold,
repeat behind.

Repeat steps
41–50 on the
right.

51

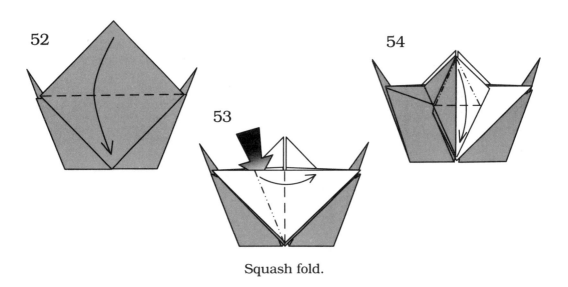

52

53

Squash fold.

54

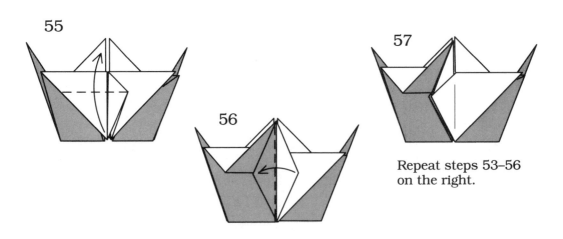

55

56

57

Repeat steps 53–56
on the right.

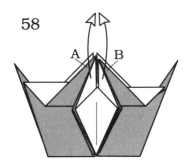

58

Pull A and B up.

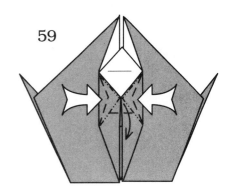

59

A three dimensional figure.

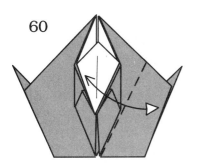

60

Fold and unfold.

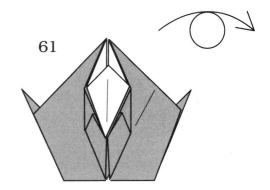

61

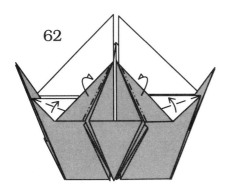

62

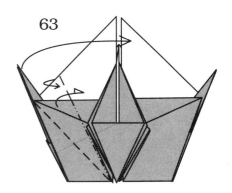

63

Crimp fold.

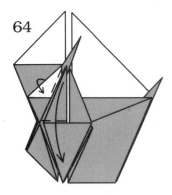

64

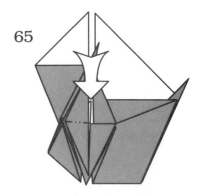

65

Remember when the center was sunk (in step 32)? Sink this little triangular flap inside the sunken center.

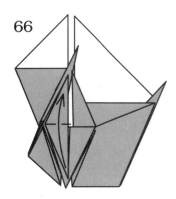

66

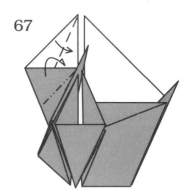

67

Reverse fold.

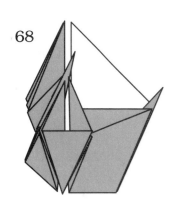

68

Repeat steps 60–67 on the right.

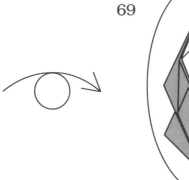

69

Montroll's Insect Base

Weevil

The weevil is a member of the the snout beetle family. It has a hard body and a long head pointing downward. This insect is a pest which does much damage to grain, cotton, nut, and other crops. It is about 1/16 to 1/2 an inch long. Most are gray, black, or brown, but some are bright blue and green.

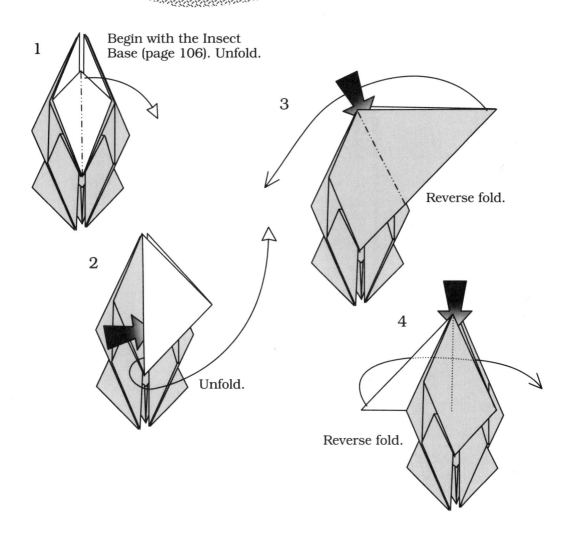

1 Begin with the Insect Base (page 106). Unfold.

2 Unfold.

3 Reverse fold.

4 Reverse fold.

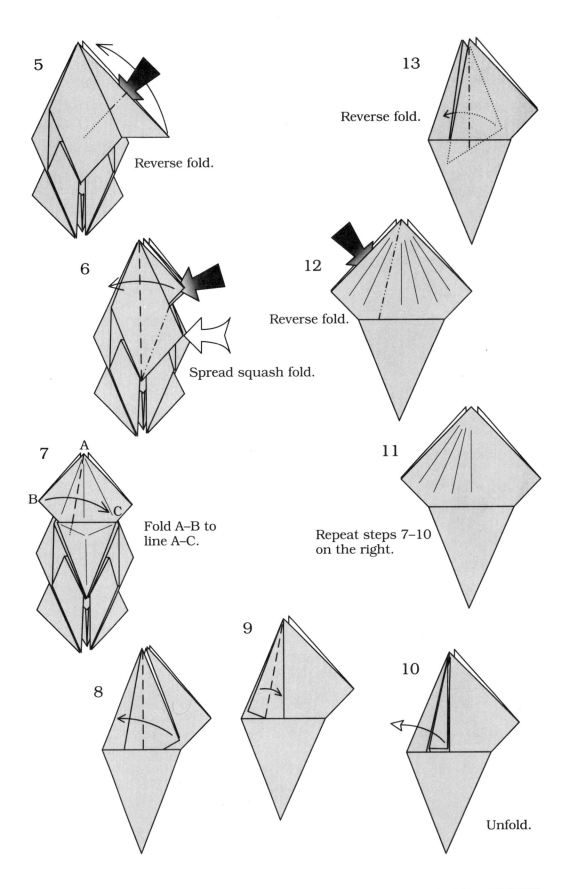

5 Reverse fold.

6 Spread squash fold.

7 Fold A–B to line A–C.

A

B C

8

9

10 Unfold.

11 Repeat steps 7–10 on the right.

12 Reverse fold.

13 Reverse fold.

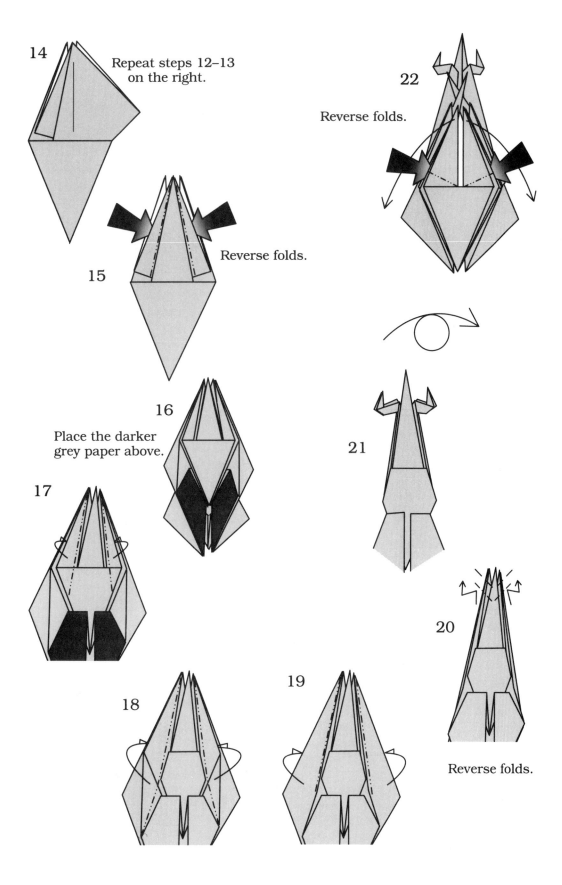

14 Repeat steps 12–13 on the right.

15 Reverse folds.

16 Place the darker grey paper above.

17

18

19

20 Reverse folds.

21

22 Reverse folds.

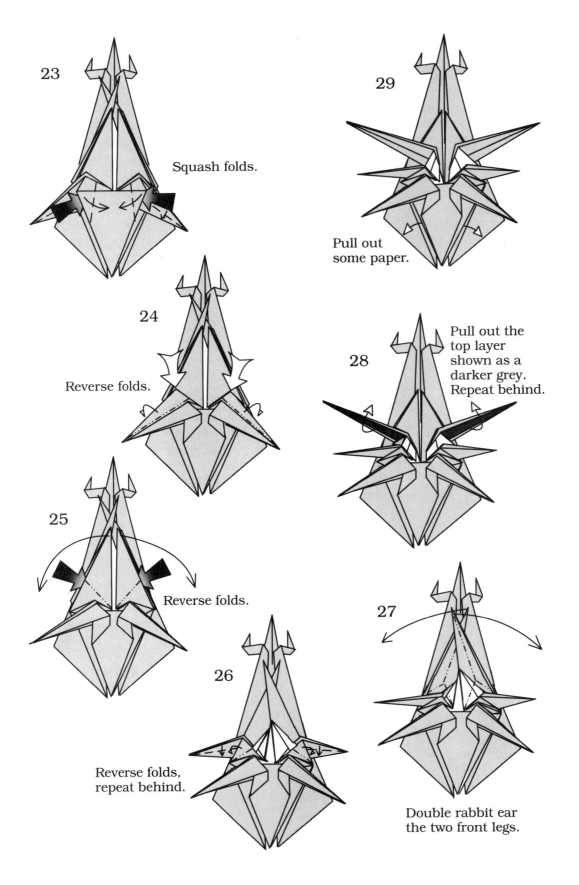

23   Squash folds.

24   Reverse folds.

25   Reverse folds.

26   Reverse folds, repeat behind.

27   Double rabbit ear the two front legs.

28   Pull out the top layer shown as a darker grey. Repeat behind.

29   Pull out some paper.

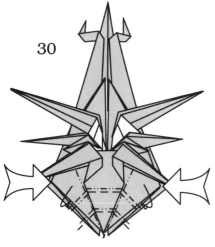

30

Shape the tail.

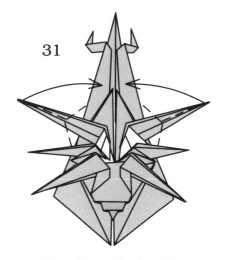

31

Rabbit ear the front legs.

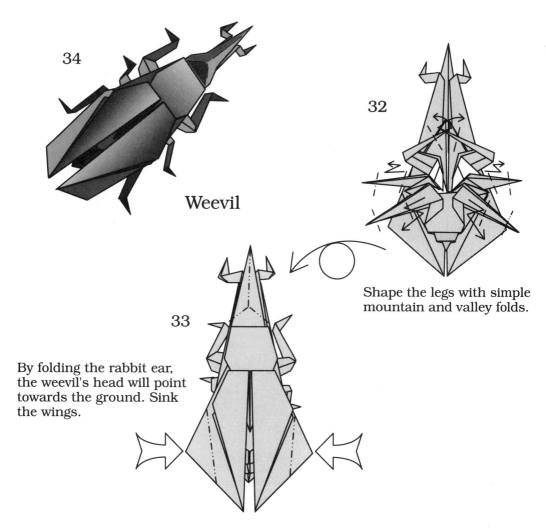

34

Weevil

32

Shape the legs with simple mountain and valley folds.

33

By folding the rabbit ear, the weevil's head will point towards the ground. Sink the wings.

Asparagus Beetle

This is a species of the leaf beetle family. The adult and its larvae cause much damage to the asparagus plant. The adults hibernate in old asparagus stalks. In the spring they come out and feed on the young shoots of the new asparagus. Then the female lays tiny black eggs on the stalk. The beetles, about six millimeters long, are blue and black and have yellow spots on their wings, and have a reddish thorax.

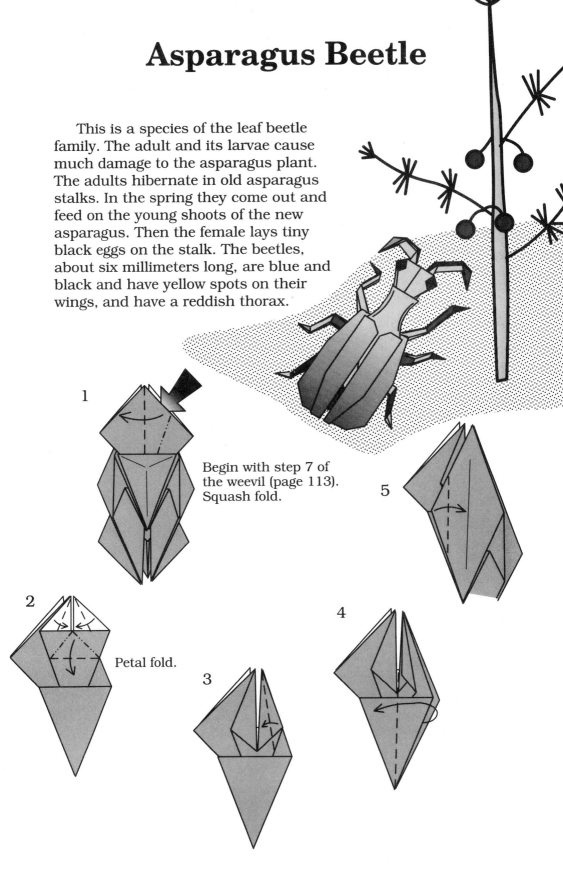

1

Begin with step 7 of the weevil (page 113). Squash fold.

5

2

Petal fold.

3

4

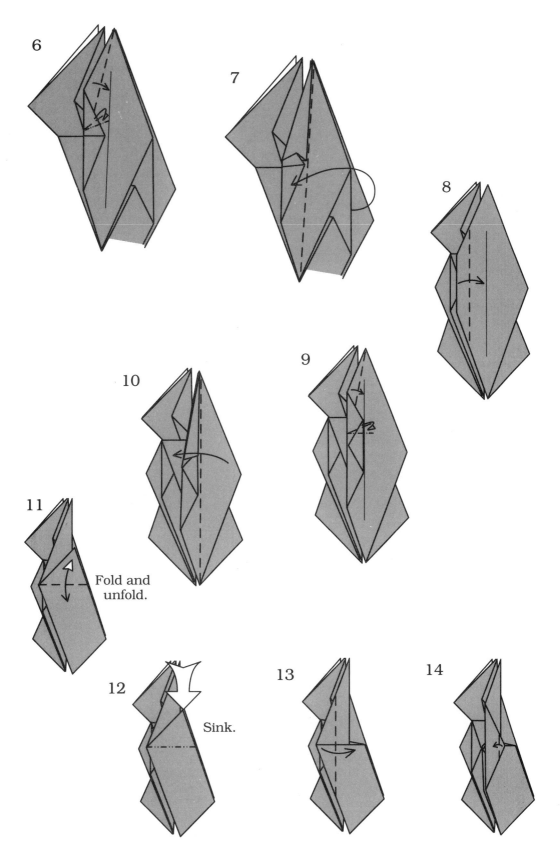

6

7

8

9

10

11

Fold and
unfold.

12

Sink.

13

14

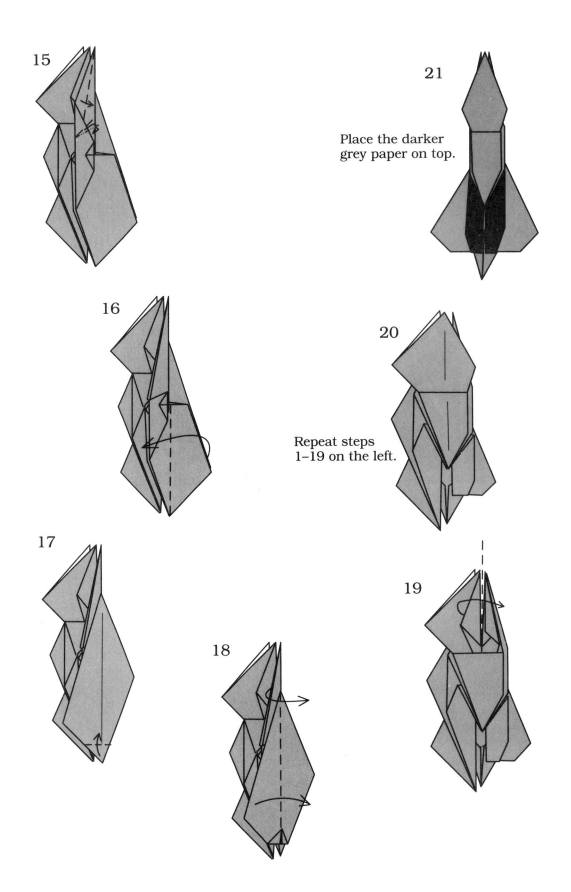

15

16

17

18

19

20

Repeat steps
1–19 on the left.

21

Place the darker
grey paper on top.

ORIGAMI SCULPTURES

22

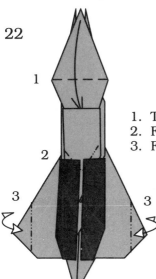

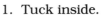

1. Tuck inside.
2. Fold behind.
3. Fold behind and unfold.

23

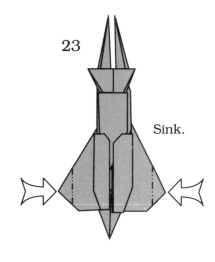

Sink.

26

24

Head.

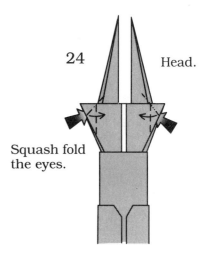

Squash fold the eyes.

Asparagus beetle

Fold the legs and tail as in the weevil (steps 22–32 of the weevil) but treat the front legs as the other ones (that is, omit steps 28 and 31).

25

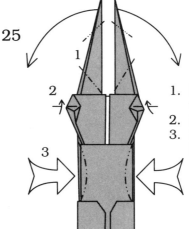

1. Shape the antennae with reverse folds.
2. Fold the eyes.
3. Make the neck three dimensional.

Panda

The Giant Panda is a rare animal found in dense bamboo jungles in Western China and Tibet at elevations of 6000 to 14000 feet. Adults are about six feet long and weigh 300 pounds. In its environment of snow and black rocks, its white and black coloring acts as a camoflauge. It is agile and can climb trees. This nocturnal mammal spends more than half its day eating large amounts of bamboo shoots, other plants, and sometimes small animals.

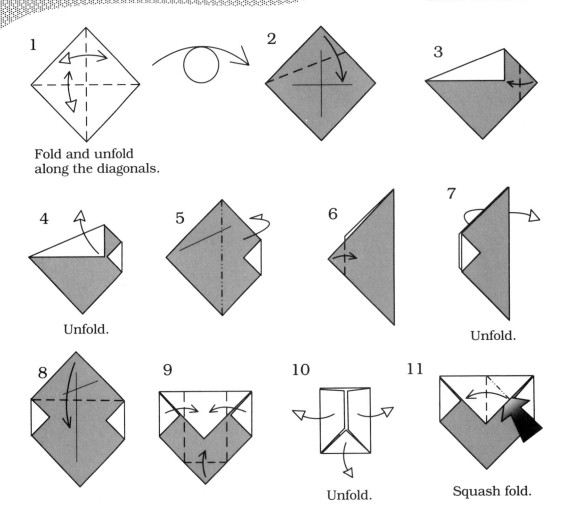

1

Fold and unfold along the diagonals.

2

3

4

Unfold.

5

6

7

Unfold.

8

9

10

Unfold.

11

Squash fold.

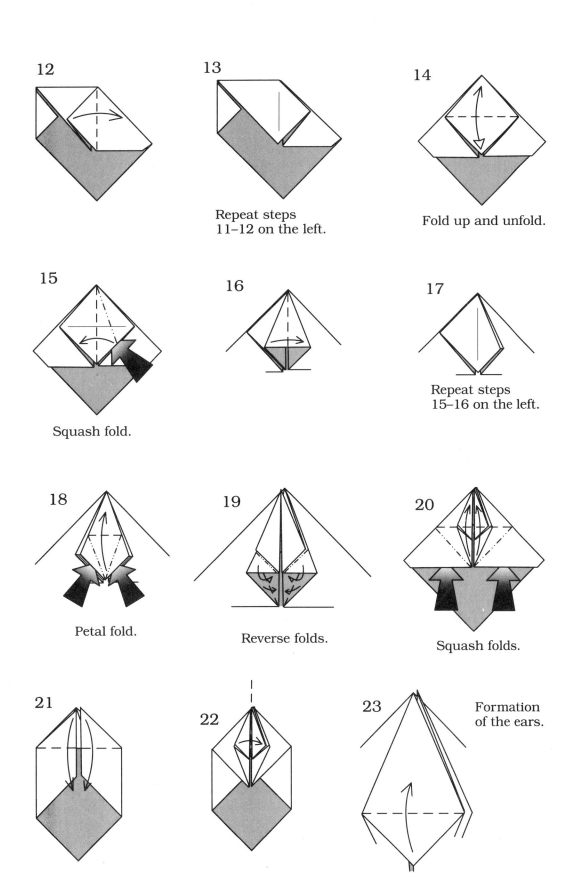

12

13

Repeat steps
11–12 on the left.

14

Fold up and unfold.

15

Squash fold.

16

17

Repeat steps
15–16 on the left.

18

Petal fold.

19

Reverse folds.

20

Squash folds.

21

22

23

Formation
of the ears.

24

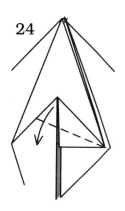

25

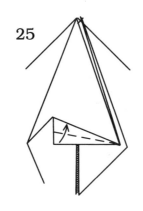

26

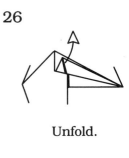

Unfold.

27

Repeat steps
24–26 on the left.

28

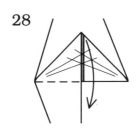

29

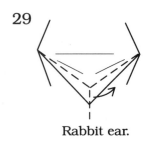

Rabbit ear.

30

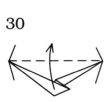

31

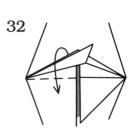

This fold is similar
to a rabbit ear.

32

33

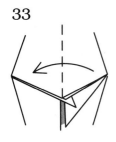

34

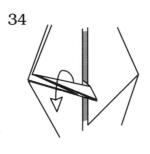

Unlock some paper.

35

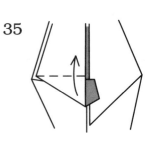

36

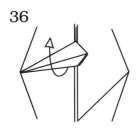

Unlock some paper.

37

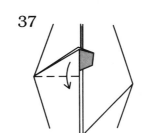

38

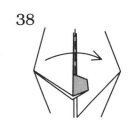

39

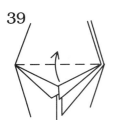

40

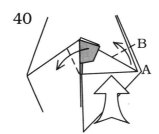

Squash fold so A
falls along line A–B.

41

42

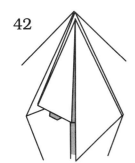

Form the other ear (repeat
steps 22–41 on the right).

43

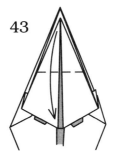

44

Unfold.

45

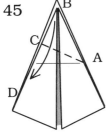

Using A as a guide,
fold B down so it will
be on the line C–D.

46

Unfold.

47

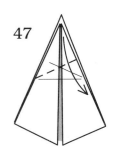

48

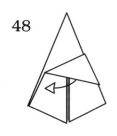

Pull out some paper.

49

Squash fold.

50

Pull out some paper.

51

52

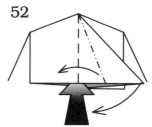

Squash fold.

53

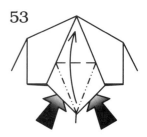

Petal fold.

54

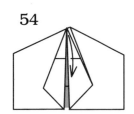

55

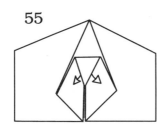

Pull out some paper.

56

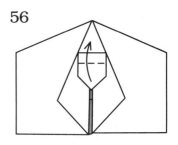

Formation of the nose.

57

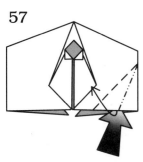

Squash fold to begin forming the eyes.

58

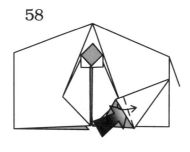

Squash fold.

59

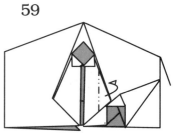

Repeat steps 57–59 on the left.

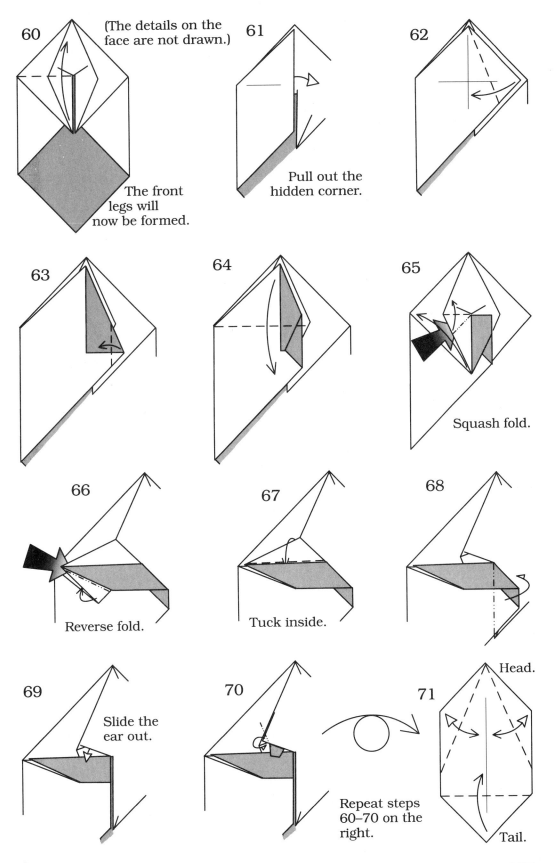

60 (The details on the face are not drawn.)

The front legs will now be formed.

61 Pull out the hidden corner.

62

63

64

65 Squash fold.

66 Reverse fold.

67 Tuck inside.

68

69 Slide the ear out.

70 Repeat steps 60–70 on the right.

71 Head.

Tail.

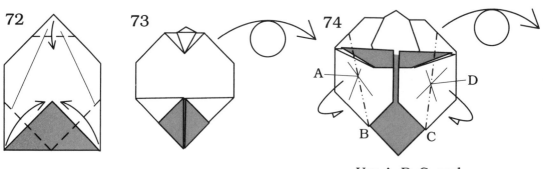

72

73

74

Use A, B, C, and
D as guides.

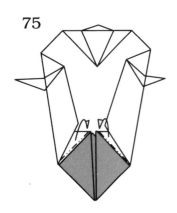

75

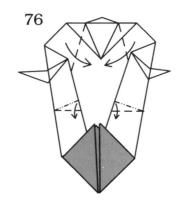

76

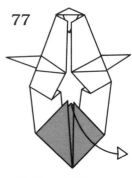

77

Pull out the
hidden corner.

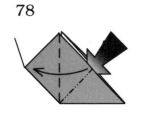

78

Squash fold.

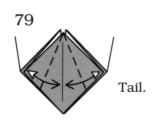

79

Tail.

Fold and unfold.

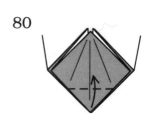

80

81

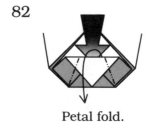

82

Petal fold.

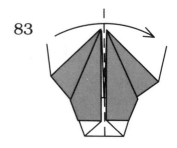

83

84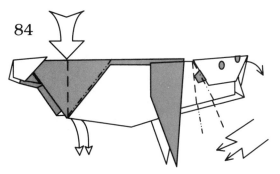

Fold the back legs down
and crimp fold the neck.

85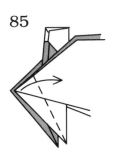

Repeat behind.

86

Reverse fold.

87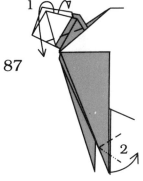

1. Outside reverse fold the tail.
2. Pull some paper out to form
   the foot. Repeat behind.

88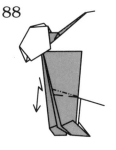

Crimp fold.
Repeat behind.

89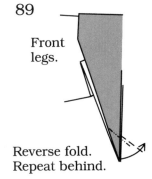

Front
legs.

Reverse fold.
Repeat behind.

90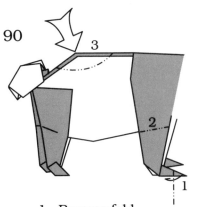

1. Reverse fold.
   Repeat behind.
2. Bend at the knee.
   Repeat behind.
3. Shape the back.

91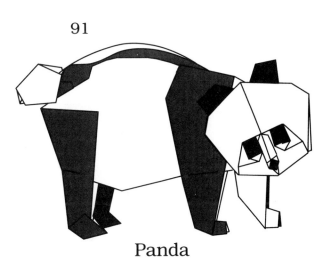

Panda

Elephant

The largest and most powerful living land animals, elephants are six to eleven feet tall and can weigh six tons or more. The trunk is an enlongated upper lip and nose. Elephants use their trunks for gathering food, drinking, smelling, fighting, throwing dust and water over their bodies, and making trumpeting sounds. They wave their trunks around to pick up faint smells.

Elephants live in Asian and African tropics and travel in herds of a hundred or more. They eat about 500 pounds of leaves, twigs, roots, and fruits and drink 50 gallons of water a day. They can run at 25 miles an hour and are good swimmers. Though large and powerful they are gentle and graceful.

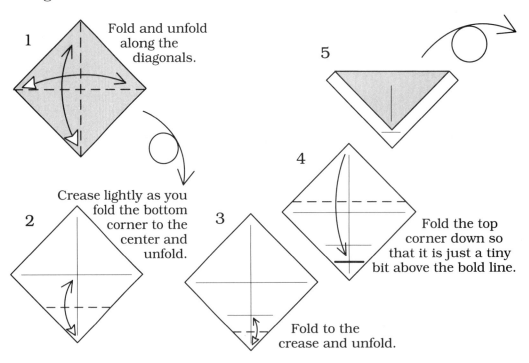

1 Fold and unfold along the diagonals.

2 Crease lightly as you fold the bottom corner to the center and unfold.

3 Fold to the crease and unfold.

4 Fold the top corner down so that it is just a tiny bit above the bold line.

5

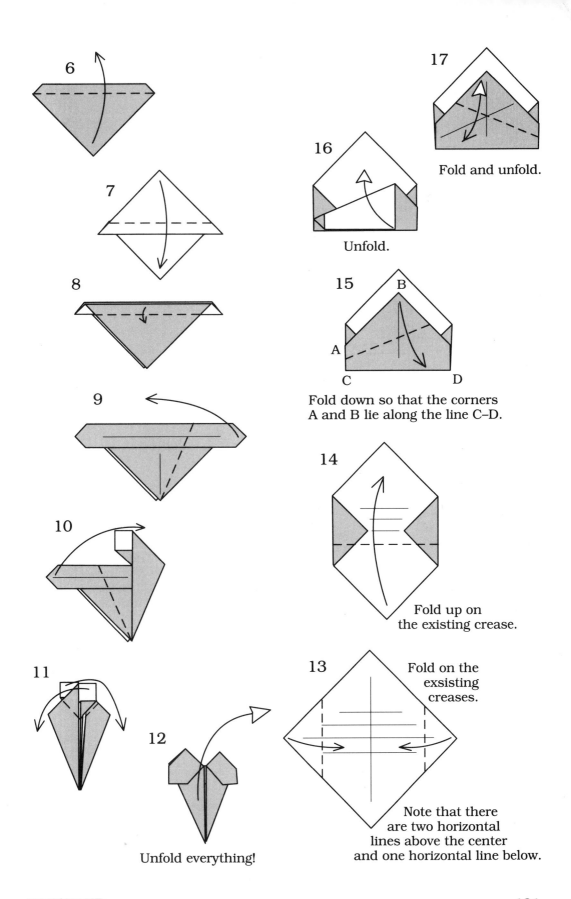

6

7

8

9

10

11

12

Unfold everything!

13

Fold on the exsisting creases.

Note that there are two horizontal lines above the center and one horizontal line below.

14

Fold up on the existing crease.

15

B

A

C   D

Fold down so that the corners A and B lie along the line C–D.

16

Unfold.

17

Fold and unfold.

ELEPHANT   **131**

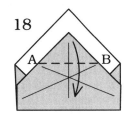

18

Use A and B as guides.

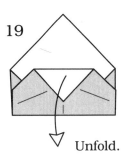

19

Unfold.

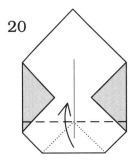

20

Use the hidden corner as a guide.

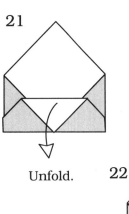

21

Unfold.

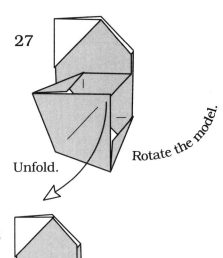

27

Unfold.   Rotate the model.

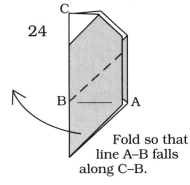

26

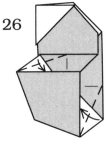

25

Squash fold.

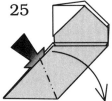

24

C

B   A

Fold so that line A–B falls along C–B.

22

Fold down and unfold.

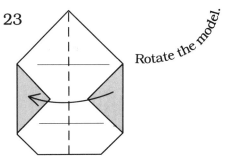

23

Rotate the model.

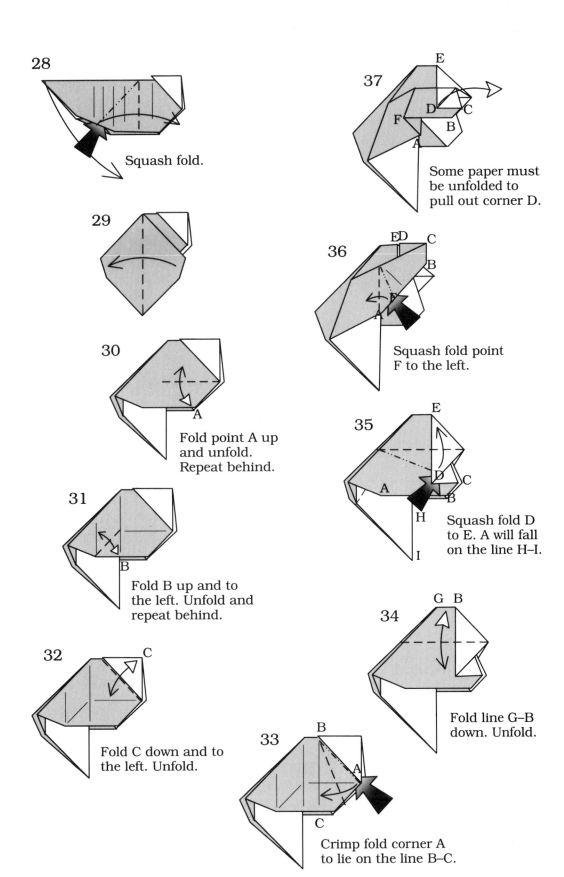

28

Squash fold.

29

30

Fold point A up
and unfold.
Repeat behind.

31

Fold B up and to
the left. Unfold and
repeat behind.

32

Fold C down and to
the left. Unfold.

33

Crimp fold corner A
to lie on the line B–C.

37

Some paper must
be unfolded to
pull out corner D.

36

Squash fold point
F to the left.

35

Squash fold D
to E. A will fall
on the line H–I.

34

Fold line G–B
down. Unfold.

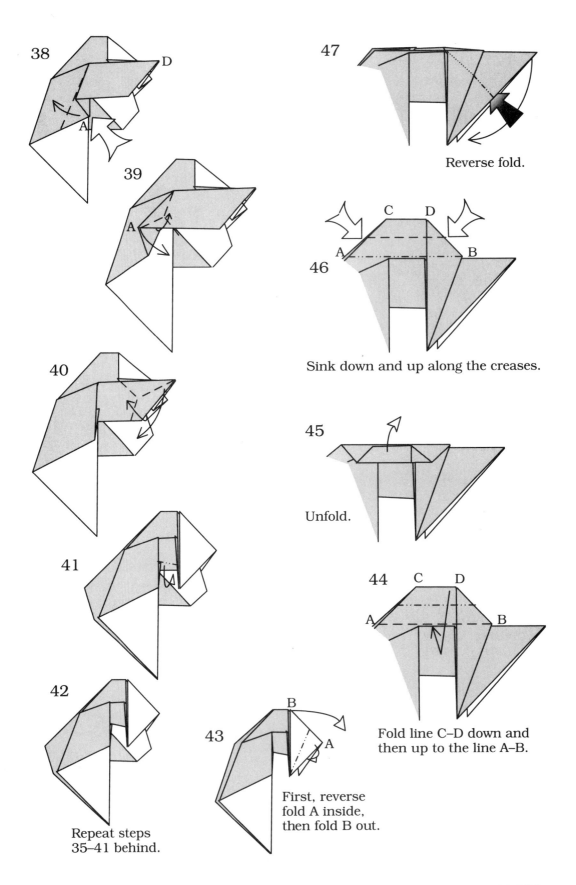

38

39

40

41

42

Repeat steps
35–41 behind.

43

B

A

First, reverse
fold A inside,
then fold B out.

47

Reverse fold.

46

C   D

A   B

Sink down and up along the creases.

45

Unfold.

44

C   D

A   B

Fold line C–D down and
then up to the line A–B.

48

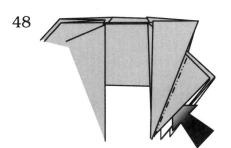

Reverse fold, repeat behind.

49

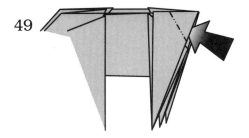

Reverse fold.

50

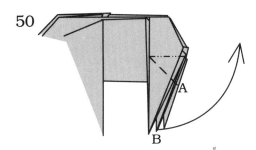

Crimp fold the tail.

51

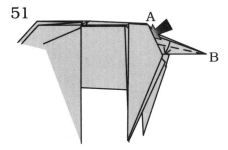

Thin the tail using a small
reverse fold by the base of
the tail. Repeat behind.

55

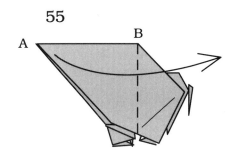

54

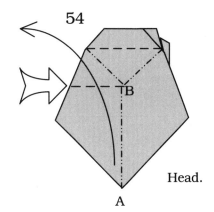

Head.

53

52

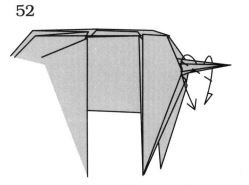

Outside reverse fold the tail.

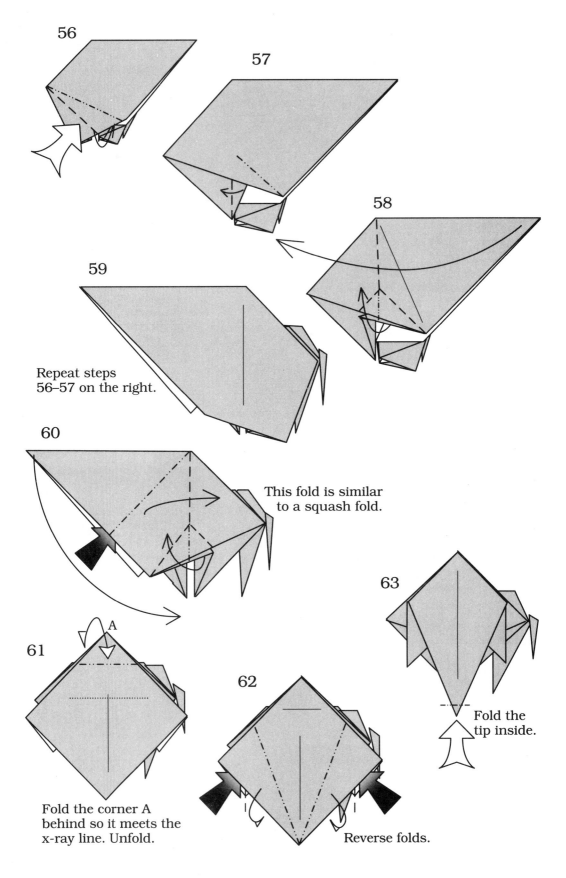

56

57

58

59

Repeat steps
56–57 on the right.

60

This fold is similar
to a squash fold.

63

Fold the
tip inside.

61

A

62

Fold the corner A
behind so it meets the
x-ray line. Unfold.

Reverse folds.

64

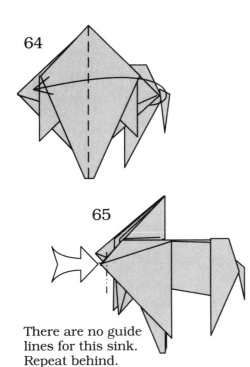

65

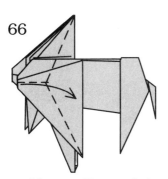

There are no guide
lines for this sink.
Repeat behind.

66

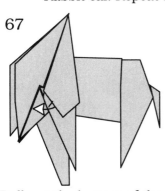

Rabbit ear. Repeat behind.

67

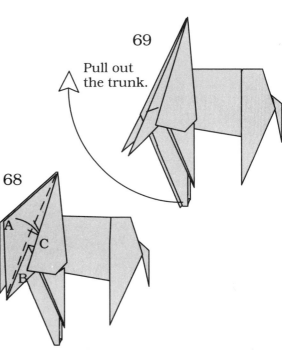

Pull out the bottom of the
ears. (Repeat behind.)
Perhaps you can skip this
step since it is really easier to
go from step 66 to 68 directly!

68

A

C

B

Fold the layer A
above B but below
C. Repeat behind.

71

Squash fold.

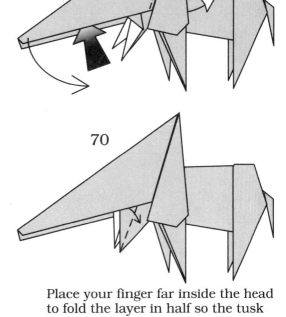

70

Place your finger far inside the head
to fold the layer in half so the tusk
will be white. Repeat behind.

69

Pull out
the trunk.

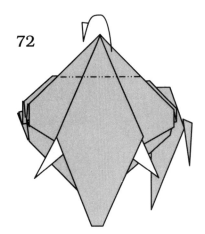

72

Tuck along the crease.

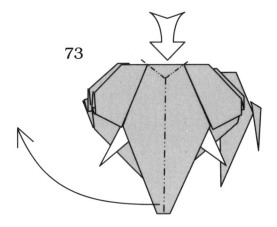

73

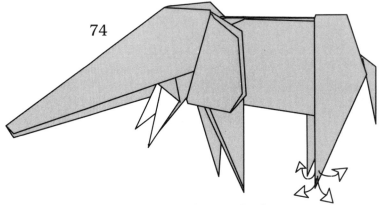

74

Spread and flatten the feet.

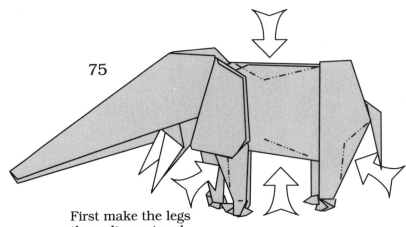

75

First make the legs
three dimensional,
then the body.

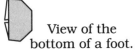

View of the
bottom of a foot.

ORIGAMI SCULPTURES

76

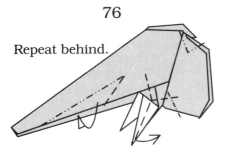

Repeat behind.

Rabbit ear the tusks.

77

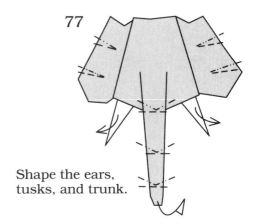

Shape the ears, tusks, and trunk.

78

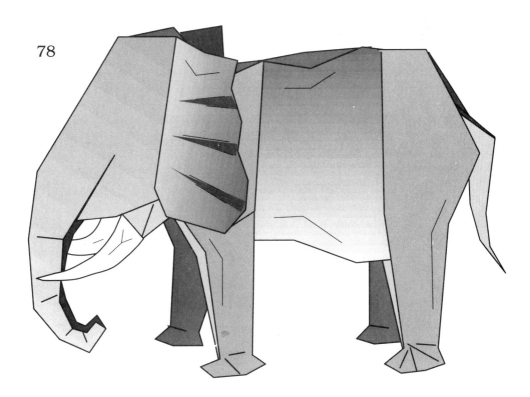

Elephant

Basic Folds

Rabbit Ear.

To fold a rabbit ear, one corner is folded in half and laid down to a side.

See steps 6–16 of the swan (page 12) for a detailed folding method.

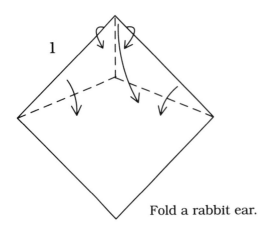

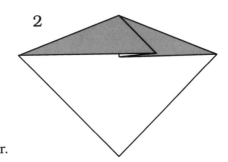

Fold a rabbit ear.

Double Rabbit Ear.

If you were to bend a straw you would be doing the double rabbit ear. This fold is commonly used to form legs.

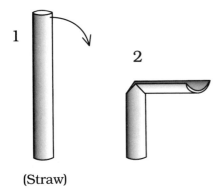

(Straw)

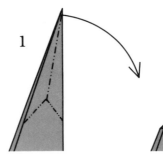

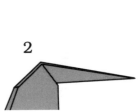

Double rabbit ear.

ORIGAMI SCULPTURES

Place Your Finger Here.

Several kinds of folds use this arrow. It is placed between layers of paper and shows where to place your finger to accomplish the fold. Several examples follow.

Squash fold.

In a squash fold, some paper is opened and then made flat. The shaded arrow shows where to place your finger.

1

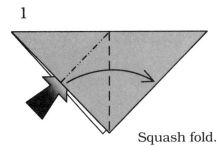

Squash fold.

2

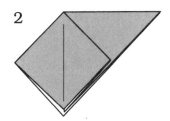

Petal Fold.

In a petal fold, one point is folded up while two opposite sides meet each other.

For a detailed explanation of the petal fold, see steps 4–9 of the goose (page 39).

1

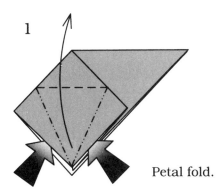

Petal fold.

2

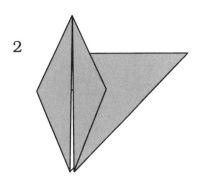

Inside Reverse Fold.

In an inside reverse fold, some paper is folded between layers. Here are two examples.

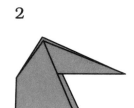

Reverse fold.

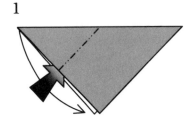

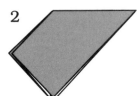

Reverse fold.

Outside Reverse Fold.

Much of the paper must be unfolded to make an outside reverse fold.

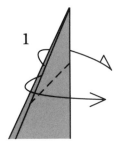

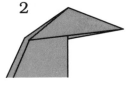

Outside reverse fold.

Crimp Fold.

A crimp fold is a combination of two reverse folds.

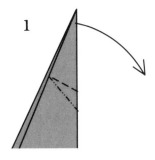

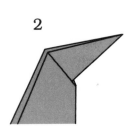

Crimp fold.

ORIGAMI SCULPTURES

Push In Arrow.

This arrow is usually used for sink folds and three dimensional folding.

Sink Fold.

In a sink fold, some of the paper which contain no edges is folded inside. To do this fold, much of the model must be unfolded.

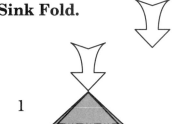

1

2

Sink.

Three Dimensional Folding.

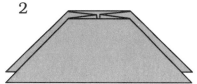

In several animals, the last step is to make them three dimensional by pushing in some paper.

1

2

Spread Squash Fold.

A cross between a squash fold and sink fold, some paper in the center is spread apart and then made flat.

1

2

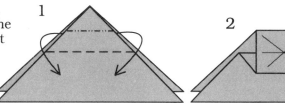

Spread squash fold.